IMAGES
of America

BELLEFONTE

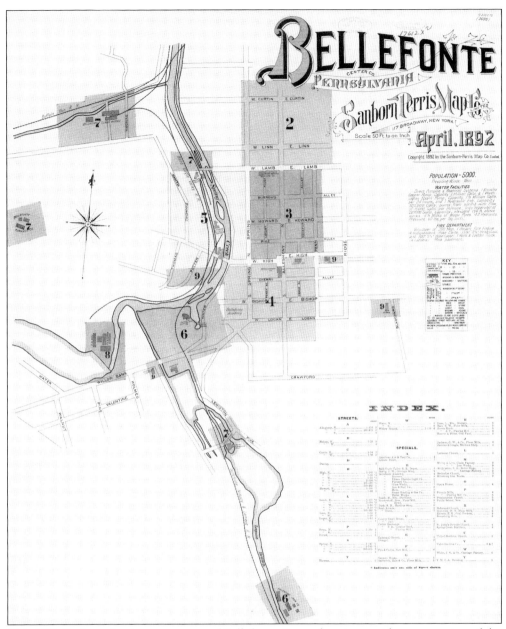

This 1892 Sanborn fire insurance map of Bellefonte, Pennsylvania, provides an overview of the town's layout and identifies major thoroughfares and selected significant buildings throughout the downtown area. (Courtesy of the Library of Congress.)

ON THE COVER: Families from Bellefonte, the surrounding countryside, and sometimes even from farther afield often gathered together for Sunday school picnics, family reunions, and other festive occasions. These special events were held at local churches, family picnic areas, and public parks such as Hecla Park. This undated photograph shows one such well-attended outdoor event held near Bellefonte. (Marsha Ann Tate.)

IMAGES
of America

BELLEFONTE

Marsha Ann Tate and Earl Houser

ARCADIA
PUBLISHING

Copyright © 2022 by Marsha Ann Tate and Earl Houser
ISBN 987-1-4671-0866-9

Published by Arcadia Publishing
Charleston, South Carolina

Printed in the United States of America

Library of Congress Control Number: 2022937401

For all general information, please contact Arcadia Publishing:
Telephone 843-853-2070
Fax 843-853-0044
E-mail sales@arcadiapublishing.com
For customer service and orders:
Toll-Free 1-888-313-2665

Visit us on the Internet at www.arcadiapublishing.com

*In memory of our parents, Barbara and Andrew J. Tate
and Joanne and Earl Houser. Their enduring
love and support made this all possible.*

CONTENTS

ACKNOWLEDGMENTS

The authors would like to thank the following individuals and organizations for their assistance with this project: Bellefonte Moose Lodge No. 206, the Centre County Library and Historical Museum, Barbara Coopey, Justin Houser, Plumbs Drug Store, Diane and Don Shaffer, and our editors at Arcadia Publishing.

Unless otherwise noted, all images are from the collection of Marsha Ann Tate.

INTRODUCTION

Nestled in the Nittany Valley, two and a half miles from the geographic center of the commonwealth of Pennsylvania, the quaint community of Bellefonte, the county seat of Centre County, offers a bountiful historical tableau. Founded in 1795 by James Dunlop and his son-in-law James Harris, Bellefonte quickly grew in economic, industrial, and political prominence during the 1800s owing to its central location within Pennsylvania's ironmaking region.

Bellefonte's rarefied status was evidenced by the fact that despite having less than 5,000 inhabitants, five Pennsylvania governors, along with future governors of California and Kansas, claimed Bellefonte as their birthplace or long-term residence.

Bellefonte's picturesque Victorian architecture reflected its economic prosperity and distinguished residents. During the mid- to late 1800s, Bellefonte's wealthy denizens built an impressive array of sizeable multistory public buildings and private residences that lined the downtown streets. These structures, designed by noted architects of the day, exemplified the beauty and ornate craftmanship of Victorian architecture, influenced by such styles as Georgian, Greek Revival, Italianate, Second Empire, Queen Anne, Gothic, and Georgian Revival.

Bellefonte's hotels, such as the Bush House and the Brockerhoff, also reflected the affluence of the town's leading citizens. Similarly, government buildings, including the armory, county courthouse, jail, and public schools, reaffirmed Bellefonte's status.

Despite Bellefonte's rich history and Victorian splendor, the town gradually faded into the shadows in the decades following the founding of the nearby Farmer's High School of Pennsylvania (now the Pennsylvania State University) in 1855 and the town of State College, which sprang up around the school.

Bellefonte chronicles a century of the town's distinguished past—from 1876 to 1976—via a combination of vintage photographs and other sundry artifacts. Each chapter of the book focuses on a specific aspect of Bellefonte's history. In addition to discussing oft-mentioned historical points of interest and famous residents, this book also provides insights into the lives and pastimes of the area's working-class residents, who have often been overlooked in other histories of the community.

Chapter one provides a brief historical background of Bellefonte, along with a tour of Bellefonte's exemplary array of Victorian architecture through photographs of selected public buildings, private residences, hotels, and government-owned facilities.

From Centre County's earliest settlement in the 1790s, farming ranked as its foremost industry, with ironmaking later joining farming as an economic mainstay, especially for Bellefonte. However, ironmaking's significance waned throughout the second half of the 19th century, and by the early 1900s, the area's once flourishing industry had virtually vanished. However, as ironmaking declined, new industries were established to fill the void. These included the Pennsylvania Match Factory, a manufacturer of wooden matches, and the Titan Metal Company, a manufacturer of brass products, with both firms becoming nationwide leaders in their respective product lines. Likewise, the limestone quarries and mines scattered throughout the Nittany Valley yield some of the highest-quality limestone products in the world, making Bellefonte lime a valuable commodity in both the domestic and international marketplaces.

As Centre County's largest community in the 1800s and its county seat, Bellefonte offered residents and visitors a plethora of dining, shopping, and entertainment options, with most of its establishments owned and operated by local families. Diners could choose from chef-prepared cuisine at the Bush House or other formal dining establishments or opt for simpler fare from one of the many family restaurants that dotted Allegheny and High Streets. Bellefonte businesses also offered customers a wide range of clothing, groceries, foods, and household goods, together with other merchandise and services. Dentists, physicians, and pharmacies were also located downtown. Chapter two highlights selected major industries and businesses in and around Bellefonte.

Bellefonte's populace worshipped at a variety of mainline Protestant churches throughout the town, including the First Presbyterian Church, St. John's Episcopal Church, and the Trinity United Methodist Church, among others. The St. Paul African Methodist Episcopal Church, constructed prior to the US Civil War, and its congregation also played a unique role in the religious and cultural life of Bellefonte and Centre County. Likewise, St. John the Evangelist Catholic Church served as the religious and cultural center for Irish, Italian, and Slavic immigrant families who settled in Bellefonte and the vicinity. Lastly, numerous Bellefonte residents were active in the Centre County Sunday School Association and similar religious organizations. Chapter three provides a century-long photographic exploration of faith, family, and friends in Bellefonte.

Both private and public educational facilities have played important roles in Bellefonte's history. In 1805, Bellefonte's founders established the Bellefonte Academy, a private preparatory school. Over time, the academy gained renown as one of Pennsylvania's most prestigious educational institutions of its kind. However, during the 1930s, the school fell victim to the Great Depression and closed its doors. Over the years, various public school facilities were also constructed in downtown Bellefonte and its environs. Chapter four explores selected public primary and secondary schools in the Bellefonte area and the students who attended these schools.

A number of Bellefonte's young persons were called to serve their country during World Wars I and II, the Korean conflict, and Vietnam. Chapter five salutes these service members and their families via photographs associated with these wartime eras.

Bellefonte residents could enjoy their leisure time by engaging in a host of recreational and entertainment activities. Chapter six shares photographic memories from Fisherman's Paradise, a unique aquatic facility and its nearby associated fish hatcheries, that capitalized on the area's superior trout fishing.

Beyond fishing, Bellefonte residents could enjoy a variety of entertainment options, including attending theatrical performances at the Scenic, Plaza, and Moose Theatres; participating in or viewing sporting events ranging from scholastic and community baseball games to boxing matches; competing in soapbox derby races; picnicking, roller skating, and swimming at Hecla Park; and enjoying festivals, fairs, and other activities.

Bellefonte also boasts multiple connections to the entertainment and arts worlds. For example, longtime Bellefonte barber William H. Mills was the paternal grandfather of the members of the popular Mills Brothers vocal group. Likewise, sculptor George Grey Barnard was a Bellefonte native. Chapter seven chronicles some of the popular pastimes and entertainment choices available to Bellefonte residents. In keeping with the pastimes and entertainment theme, chapter eight is devoted to the Bellefonte Banjo Band, a renowned musical organization that frequently performed at community celebrations. Likewise, chapter nine is dedicated to a Centre County institution: the Grange Encampment and Fair, an annual event beloved by generations of Bellefonte families.

Lastly, chapter ten explores vestiges of the past still visible throughout downtown Bellefonte.

We hope you enjoy travelling with us back in time for a visit to Bellefonte and its residents of the past.

One

WELCOME TO BELLEFONTE

Bellefonte-themed postcards featuring the town's notable buildings, the Big Spring, and various other sites of interest, along with humorous drawings, as exemplified by this 1920s postcard, provided an inexpensive means of promoting Bellefonte to tourists and businesses and even helped attract potential permanent residents to the central Pennsylvania community.

The three-story James Harris House on South Potter Street was built in 1795 by the residence's namesake owner. As noted in the Historic American Buildings Survey documentation for the home, "mahogany doors between the parlors and from parlors to hall were brought from the old Walnut Street Theatre in Philadelphia sometime after 1828, when the house was remodeled." (Courtesy of the Library of Congress.)

This postcard provides a bird's-eye view of downtown Bellefonte from High Street. High and Allegheny Streets have historically comprised the heart of downtown Bellefonte's business district, with the streets intersecting in front of the Centre County Courthouse in an area commonly referred to as "the Diamond."

The two-story Centre County Courthouse, constructed of limestone, was originally built in 1805, with a portico and pediment added in 1835. In 1854–1855, the structure was rebuilt, including the addition of a domed cupola. In 1906, a colonnade featuring a bronze statue of Bellefonte native and Pennsylvania's Civil War governor Andrew Gregg Curtin was erected in front of the courthouse. Three years later, the courthouse was enlarged and its interior extensively renovated.

In 1800, the Centre County Prison was established when Hudson Williams was authorized to build a prison on East High Street. In 1867, a new prison, shown on this postcard, was built on a hill behind the county courthouse. The two-story stone structure also housed the sheriff and his family. In January 1959, the prison was destroyed by a fire; it was rebuilt in 1964.

This postcard offers a view of South Allegheny Street looking down from the Diamond in front of the Centre County Courthouse. The first building on the left is the Reynolds Bank building, constructed by Maj. William Frederick Reynolds in 1887 as a bank and reconstructed in 1889 following several fires. It was later known as First National Bank and the Bellefonte Trust Company.

The four-story Temple Court Building on South Allegheny Street parallel to the Centre County Courthouse and adjacent to the Reynolds bank building was designed by local builder John Robert Cole (1850–1916) and constructed in 1894. As its name suggests, the building's occupants traditionally included attorneys and insurance agencies, along with commercial businesses on the first floor.

The Brockerhoff Hotel, on South Allegheny Street at the southwest corner of the Diamond, was once the site of a log cabin tavern. The hotel was constructed in 1865 by German-born businessman Henry Brockerhoff (1794–1878) at a reported cost of $50,000. In the 1890s, the hotel was redesigned by John Robert Cole, who added a fourth floor and a new roof design.

Extending east and west through Bellefonte and crossing Allegheny Street at the Diamond, High Street was home to several banks and the YMCA, along with a variety of retail establishments, restaurants, and the town's principal indoor entertainment venues. West High Street also boasted the Bush Arcade (large building with cupola at center), which housed various businesses, along with the spacious Bush House Hotel (left), built parallel to Spring Creek directly across from the train station.

13

The fabled Big Spring has served as the municipal water source for Bellefonte and nearby communities throughout the town's history. According to local lore, during a mid-1790s visit to the spring, exiled French statesman Charles-Maurice de Talleyrand reputedly suggested to his hostess that the surrounding area be called *Bellefonte* (French for "beautiful spring"). Although the quaint story's veracity is questionable, the importance of the Big Spring to Bellefonte's growth and development is indisputable. The postcard above shows the spring and waterworks in the early 1900s. The pumphouse pictured on the postcard below was built in 1926. A covering was eventually placed over the Big Spring as a protective measure.

Bellefonte's Famous Spring, Bellefonte, Pa.

By the mid-1880s, passenger trains running north, south, east, and west made daily stops at Bellefonte. The postcard above shows the Pennsylvania Railroad Station on West High Street. The larger building beside the train station housed the Bellefonte branch of the Lauderbach-Garber Company, a wholesale grocery firm. Many travelers stayed at the Bush House (below), a hotel built across the street from the railroad station in 1868–1869 by lawyer and developer Daniel Griffen Bush, a Bradford County, Pennsylvania, native and a former schoolteacher who ventured to Bellefonte in 1856 to complete his preparation for the bar. Over the years, the Bush House's notable guests included Thomas A. Edison, Henry Ford, and Amelia Earhart. In 1928, William J. Emerich purchased the hotel and renamed it the Penn Belle Hotel. The carriage of the Bush House's primary competitor, the Brockerhoff Hotel, appears in the image above.

The Bush House, Bellefonte, Pa.

556-7

In this World War I–era photograph, Coleville sisters Winifred and Florence Crawford pose on the steps of the First National Bank Building on the corner of High and Allegheny Streets at the northwest corner of the Diamond. The building, constructed in 1872, was rebuilt in 1889 following a fire a year earlier. The sign in the background is for Montgomery & Co. Menswear.

John G. Dubbs was a dealer in wagons ("Brookville wagons a specialty"), buggies, farm machinery, pumps, and other related goods. Dubbs's office and warehouse were on Dunlop Street, with his clientele including town residents and farmers living on the outskirts of Bellefonte. In addition to advertising cards, Dubbs ran ads in the *Democratic Watchman*, with a June 1911 ad announcing a giveaway of "wagon and machine umbrellas . . . absolutely free."

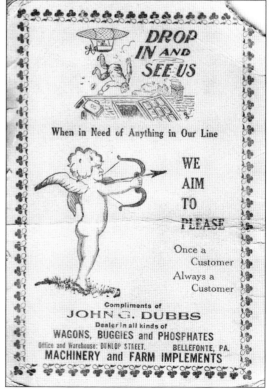

The G.C. Murphy five and dime store was a popular shopping destination for Bellefonte residents. Founded in McKeesport, Pennsylvania, in 1906 by George Clinton Murphy, the retailer grew to a chain of more than 500 stores. The Bellefonte location initially consisted of a one-room store in a different building. In 1936, the store moved and expanded its sales space to encompass both the first floor of the Brockerhoff House on Allegheny Street and an extension built along High Street. Murphy's sold everything from clothing and candy to craft and sewing materials, toys, records, and even live pets, including goldfish and occasionally live chicks. At right is a complimentary February 1938 Simplicity Fashion Forecast distributed to customers. The 1960s image below shows employee Joanne Houser working at the Bellefonte store.

Shur-on Glasses
Quality Beyond Question

C. D. CASEBEER
REGISTERED OPTOMETRIST

Established 1906   BELLEFONTE, PA.

A variety of medical professionals maintained offices in downtown Bellefonte, as evidenced by this 1920s ad from optometrist C.D. Casebeer. According to a report in the February 5, 1926, *Democratic Watchman*, Casebeer had purchased "the W. S. Katz property, adjoining Petrikin Hall" (on West High Street) where he intended to "open an optical parlor on the first floor and" occupy "the second floor as an apartment for himself and family."

In the 1950s, Valley View resident Earl Houser Sr. shops at a downtown drugstore. Over the years, numerous drugstores have operated in Bellefonte, including Dr. Kirk's, F. Potts Green, Zeller & Co., Gray Drug Stores Inc. (1 South Allegheny Street), Parrish Drug Store (114 North Allegheny Street), White Brothers (105 North Allegheny Street), Mott Drug Company, and Widman's. (Earl Houser Jr.)

Residences of three Ex Governors

Residence of A. G. Curtin

Residence of James A. Beaver

Residence of D. H. Hastings

Five Pennsylvania governors and two governors of other states were born in or resided in Bellefonte. This postcard depicts the Bellefonte residences of three former Pennsylvania governors: Andrew Curtin (1815/1817–1894), governor from January 15, 1861, until January 15, 1867 (top); James Addams Beaver (1837–1914), governor from January 18, 1887, until January 20, 1891 (bottom left); and Daniel Hartman Hastings (1849–1903), governor from January 15, 1895, to January 17, 1899 (bottom right).

Andrew Curtin was born in Bellefonte in April 1815 or 1817, the son of iron manufacturer Roland Curtin and his second wife, the former Jean Gregg (1791–1854), daughter of US senator Andrew Gregg. Curtin, a lawyer by profession, was Pennsylvania's Civil War governor, leaving office in 1867. Thereafter, he served as minister to Russia and then as a US representative from 1881 to 1887. He died in Bellefonte on October 7, 1894. (Courtesy of the Library of Congress.)

William Bigler (1813 or 1814–1880) moved to Bellefonte in the 1820s to work for his older brother John, then editor of the *Centre County Democrat* (and a future governor of California). In 1833, Bigler relocated to Clearfield, Pennsylvania, where he founded the *Clearfield Democrat* and later served as a state senator (1841–1847), governor of Pennsylvania (1852–1855), and US senator (1856–1861). (Courtesy of the Library of Congress.)

The Henry S. Linn House on North Allegheny Street was built by Gen. Philip Benner for Judge Jonathan Walker, father of Pennsylvania governor Robert Walker, to try to keep him in Bellefonte. Although the ploy worked for a few years, Judge Walker eventually moved away. Upon General Benner's death in 1832, the residence was bequeathed to his daughter Mary, who later married John Blair Linn, secretary of the commonwealth under Gov. John Hartranft. The couple lived in the residence from 1871 to 1899. (Photograph by Dean E. Kennedy, courtesy of the Library of Congress.)

Two

FROM FARMS TO FACTORIES

This undated photograph shows a Bellefonte-area family posing in front of their barn. Centre County's iron manufacturers required vast amounts of timber to make charcoal for fueling furnaces and forges. Once the fertile valley lands were cleared of trees, they were often converted to farming. In fact, as of 1963, one third of Centre County's overall area remained dedicated to farming, with dairy products representing 60 percent of the farmers' total annual income.

Given the abundance of limestone in the area, private residences were frequently constructed of stone rather than wood. In this 1907–1908 photograph, Ida Tate and her four children stand beside their rural farmhouse outside of Bellefonte.

The children of Wesley W. and Ida (Love) Tate pose for a studio portrait. The children are, from left to right, (first row) Marie Love Tate (born October 21, 1904) and Teckla Isabel Tate (September 24, 1906); (second row) Rankin Dale Tate (October 22, 1899) and Andrew Jackson Tate (October 11, 1901).

During their teenage years, sisters Marie (left) and Teckla Tate, pictured above, lived with their parents and two brothers on a farm off the Bellefonte–Pleasant Gap Highway (also known as the Lewistown Turnpike, now state Route 144). The undated photograph at right shows a barefoot boy standing with a calf at a Bellefonte area farm. Every member of farm families, young and old alike, was expected to assist with farm chores, including feeding and milking the cows, sowing and harvesting crops, and other activities. Given the rigors of farm life, relatively few children remained on their family's farms; instead, they pursued jobs offering steadier incomes and regular hours at the burgeoning government and private employers throughout Centre County.

This 1920s photograph of the Teddy Lindquist residence shows a typical homestead beyond Bellefonte's town limits. Large and spacious front porches were a mainstay of these homesteads, providing a refuge from the summer heat, a viewing stand to watch the goings-on in the neighborhood, and a meeting spot for family and friends. Automobiles became an indispensable asset for rural families.

Whenever space allowed, residents of Bellefonte and other small villages throughout Centre County built small- to medium-sized backyard barns and sheds such as this one on Main Street in Pleasant Gap. The structures were variously used to shelter horses and later automobiles, store gardening implements and other equipment, and for carpentry and work shops. Rural homeowners also often raised chickens and occasionally owned a dairy cow.

This c. 1910s photograph shows a hunter standing on the porch steps of the Wesley Tate family farmhouse on the Bellefonte–Pleasant Gap Highway. Hunting and fishing were not just pastimes for farmers and working-class residents of the Bellefonte area. They also provided inexpensive and easily accessible sources of food for families. Some residents also supplemented their income by trapping muskrats and other animals.

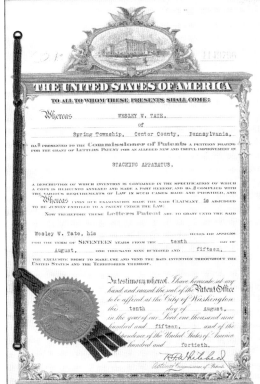

In addition to being a father and a farmer, Spring Township resident Wesley Tate was also a US patent holder. On August 10, 1915, Tate was granted patent number 1,149,796 for his invention, a stacking apparatus. He also constructed a scale model of the machine. It is not known whether a full-scale version of the apparatus was ever made.

Residents of Bellefonte and its environs frequently grew their own fruits, vegetables, herbs, and flowers. Home canned goods such as jams and jellies, juices, and meats were stored in root cellars and basements. Moreover, friends and neighbors often exchanged seeds and cuttings of plants. At left, three men work in a local garden. Below, Winifred Walters plants flowers while her daughter Joanne looks on. (Below, Earl Houser Jr.)

In the c. 1910s photograph at right, Florence Crawford (left) and three other young women pose with cooking utensils. Below, Winifred Walters washes dishes in the kitchen of her Coleville residence, with the family's coal-fired cookstove in the background. Beyond homemaking, career options for local women included working as domestic servants or housekeepers, teaching at area schools, or working in factories that employed predominantly female workforces. The shift to out-of-home employment also influenced women to forgo long hair for bobbed hairstyles. As an item in the March 19, 1926, *Democratic Watchman* noted, bobbed hair "cut the toll of industrial accidents among women workers . . . 15% in the last three years," making the trend "one of the greatest 'safety first' measures ever introduced for women workers." (Below, Earl Houser Jr.)

This cast-iron pig was produced by the Nittany Iron Company between 1902 and 1911. The company's hot-blast iron furnace, Nittany Furnace, was built on Logan Branch in Spring Township in the late 1880s on the site of the former Valentine Furnace. The Nittany Furnace went out of blast in January 1911, and like its predecessor, it was subsequently demolished. The property was then used by Titan Metal Company.

The Bellefonte area's lime industry dates to the early 1800s, coinciding with the beginning of ironmaking in the region. By 1904, the American Lime & Stone Company, a lime and stone trust under the leadership of Robert K. Cassatt, had acquired 20 tracts of land around Bellefonte, including several existing quarries and kilns. This 1920s image shows the Company's Coleville plant.

Between 1901 and 1922, American Lime & Stone Company operated nine plants in Centre County, principally north and west of Bellefonte along Spring Creek and Buffalo Run between Coleville and Milesburg. These early 1920s photographs were taken during Florence and Winifred Crawford's visit with their brother Elmer (standing at left in the image at right), a laborer at American Lime's underground mine in Coleville, which opened in 1921. From about 1867 until 1903, the Bellefonte Window Glass Company occupied the site of American Lime's Coleville plant. After the glassworks was destroyed by fire, the owners sold the property to American Lime & Stone, which then constructed its facility there.

Here are two early 1920s views of a conveyor at American Lime & Stone Company's Coleville plant. In 1922, the Charles Warner Company (later the Warner Company) assumed control of American Lime & Stone, and in 1944, Warner took over direct operations of the Coleville plant and other facilities. Since the Bellefonte area was endowed with a coveted high-grade calcium limestone, the lime industry flourished here throughout the 20th century. By the early 1960s, lime plants in the area that prepared lime for agricultural, commercial, and industrial uses included Warner Company in Coleville, National Gypsum Company along Buffalo Run Road outside of Coleville, Standard Lime & Cement Company on the outskirts of Pleasant Gap, and Fry Coal and Stone Company (formerly Whiterock) in Pleasant Gap.

Coleville is a small working-class town adjacent to the western boundary of Bellefonte along the banks of Spring Creek. The town was laid out in March 1869 by John Cole, father of local builder John Robert Cole, who had purchased several acres of land from the W.A. Thomas estate. That same year, Cole built 10 to 12 homes on the land, with the community growing to include approximately 100 homes and around 700 residents by the early 1960s. The American Lime & Stone Company's plant (later Warner Company) was at Coleville's eastern edge, with the National Gypsum Company plant several miles farther up from the town. Coleville principally consists of two main streets that form a large oval. Over the years, several schools were built in the town along with the Pilgrim Holiness Church, a tavern, and a grocery store. At right, a child stands in the front yard of the William Crawford residence in Coleville. In the c. 1920 photograph below, Florence Crawford stands on a cleared hillside near her family's Coleville home.

Pleasant Gap, Centre County's fourth largest community in the early 1960s, is approximately five miles south of Bellefonte. The village, originally known as Connelley's Gap, was on one of the county's first north-south roadways. Two limestone enterprises, Whiterock Quarries (main office shown above) and Standard Lime & Cement Company, comprised Pleasant Gap's major industries. A Pennsylvania Fish Commission hatchery nearby and the state correctional institution at Rockview provided jobs for many of the community's residents. The bustling village also included Lutheran and Methodist churches, the Logan Grange hall, the Pleasant Gap Fire Company's fire hall and carnival grounds, an American Legion post, Spring Township High School, and several restaurants, grocery stores, and other businesses. In the 1930s photograph at left, Teckla (left) and Marie Tate sit in a yard across from the Clover Farm Store on South Main Street in Pleasant Gap.

This is an undated studio portrait of Coleville resident and limestone worker William Crawford. According to US census records, His parents were both born in the Irish Free State, although nothing more is known about them. Crawford, together with his wife, children, and several other family members, lived in a two-story wood-frame home across from the American Lime & Stone Company plant.

Miles Kirk Houser (right) stands next to an unidentified man at the National Gypsum Company plant in Valley View, Benner Township. Houser, born on October 12, 1882, in Valley View, was a descendant of Jacob Houser, the founder of nearby Houserville, Pennsylvania. Miles, the youngest son of a large family, worked at the National Gypsum plant. Around 1909, he narrowly escaped death in an accident at the plant. (Earl Houser Jr.)

On June 17, 1950, National Gypsum Company's Bellefonte facility was one of two Pennsylvania mines to receive the US Bureau of Mines top safety honors for 1949. Miles Houser, then a 47-year veteran of the plant, accepted the bureau's bronze trophy on behalf of National Gypsum from Bureau of Mines director Dr. James Boyd at a ceremony held at the Penn-Belle Hotel (formerly the Bush House). The *Tyrone Daily Herald* noted that Houser had "never . . . lost time because of injuries in the last 40 years." Moreover, the Bellefonte mine had operated 234,618 man-hours in 1949 without a serious injury. (Both, Earl Houser Jr.)

The Titan Metal Company, founded by William P. Sieg in 1915, began as a small rolling mill along Logan Branch just outside of Bellefonte. Over time, the mill, dedicated to making brass and bronze rods, expanded to encompass six plants in and near Bellefonte. In 1931, Titan pioneered a Polak brass die-casting process, and during World War II, it produced brass fuse components for artillery shells, with Titan's output accounting for approximately 20 percent of the United States' total brass rod and forgings. The company also manufactured brass forgings for timing apparatus in airplanes, radar forgings, bomb components, valve assemblies for life rafts, electrical connections, and other war-related material. In the postwar era, Titan produced brass rod and welding bronze and made component parts for the plumbing, automotive, electrical appliance, radio, and other industries. In 1962, Cerro de Pasco purchased Titan Metal, with the company becoming known as the Cerro Copper and Brass Company. (Both, courtesy of the Centre County Library & Historical Museum.)

On October 15, 1952, visitors were given an opportunity to see Titan Metal Manufacturing Company's operations firsthand via tours of the facility. The open house was held in conjunction with Pennsylvania Week, a weeklong event that showcased Pennsylvania's industries. The event, held annually in September or October, was initiated by Gov. Edward Martin in 1946 in an effort "to stimulate greater pride in the past and present greatness of Pennsylvania." At left is the pamphlet distributed to visitors to the Titan plant; below is a metal souvenir given to visitors.

In this c. 1923 photograph, seven female employees of J.H. & C.K. Eagle Inc. stand near the factory on a footbridge crossing Spring Creek. The manufacturer of silk goods was headquartered in Shamokin, Pennsylvania, and operated mills in Bellefonte, Bethlehem, Edgewood, Kulpmont, Mechanicsburg, Phoenixville, Shamokin, Trevorton, and elsewhere.

The Eagle Co-Worker was a publication for workers of J.H. & C.K. Eagle Inc. The October 1923 issue included the company's dining room and cafeteria menus; news and humorous items from each of the factory locations, with Bellefonte's news labelled "Bellefonte Founts"; scores and schedules for the Eagle affiliated baseball teams; and more.

Employees of the Olde-Tyme Bakery, located at 25 ½ Cedar Alley in downtown Bellefonte, are pictured here. In August 1948, Charles M. Thompson, owner of the bakery for 20 years, sold the business to Guy S. Beaver of Lewistown. Another downtown bakery, founded in 1919 by George Kelly and later renamed Clevenstine's Bakery, was at 136 South Allegheny Street.

ARRIVAL OF MORNING MAIL FROM CLEVELAND—U. S. AIR MAIL FIELD, BELLEFONTE, PA.

On May 15, 1918, the US Post Office Department launched America's first regularly scheduled airmail route between New York City and Washington, DC, via Philadelphia. From 1919 to 1926, the Bellefonte Airfield served as an important refueling stop on the New York-to-Cleveland route. Although less than 2,000 feet in elevation, the mountains surrounding Bellefonte presented formidable and sometimes deadly obstacles to airmail pilots.

Rockview Penitentiary, now known as the Rockview Correctional Institution, is midway between Bellefonte and State College. The prison, originally a branch of the Western State Penitentiary, was constructed in 1912 on 5,000 acres formerly occupied by farms and a 936-acre state forest reserve. Rockview was self-sufficient—its food supplies were obtained via farming, with inmates predominantly making up the workforce. A large cannery, under the jurisdiction of Prison Industries, was also built on the prison grounds, with canned goods shipped to the Western State Penitentiary in Pittsburgh and other state prisons. As of June 4, 1959, there were 999 inmates and 220 employees at Rockview. The facility also housed Pennsylvania's electric chair, with the first execution taking place on February 23, 1915. By the late 1950s, an average of six inmates were executed each year at the prison.

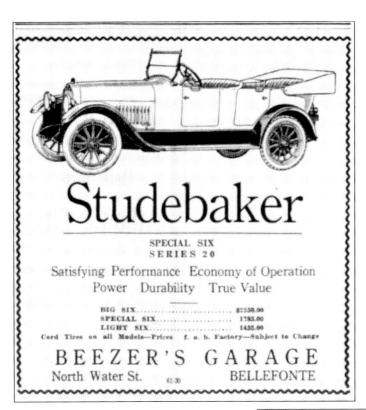

New and used vehicles, tires, and other automotive-related parts, supplies, and services were offered at various Bellefonte garages. As seen in this November 1920 *Democratic Watchman* advertisement, George A. Beezer's Garage on North Water Street specialized in Studebaker vehicles. Other garages of the era included the Bellefonte Garage (corner of West Burrows and Locust Alleys), Jodon Motor Company (South Water Street), S.H. Poorman (South Water Street), and Wion Garage (corner of South Allegheny and West Bishop Streets).

The Mallory Studio, a downtown Bellefonte photography business, captured countless Bellefonte residents on film for posterity. Individuals and families of all economic classes, attired in their best clothes, sat for portraits at the studio's Crider's Exchange location. Originally known as the Mallory Taylor Studio, the shop also provided developing services, as illustrated by this undated Mallory Studio photo envelope. Nittany Studio in the Crider Exchange building and Sager Photo were two of Bellefonte's other well-known commercial photography studios.

In 1928, brothers Ward and Carl Markle, who already operated a thriving milk route, purchased a lot in Pleasant Gap on state Route 144 and built a dairy that included a pasteurizing plant. After 1933, the dairy's product line was expanded, with machines added for making ice cream and buttermilk. Markle's Dairy delivered milk products to customers in Pleasant Gap, Bellefonte, Coleville, Centre Hall, and elsewhere.

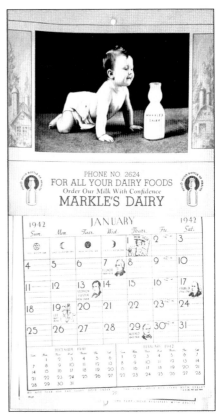

For 42 years, Jack Wilkinson owned and operated the Jack Wilkinson Inc. store at 118 North Allegheny Street in Bellefonte. The store sold office equipment, furniture, and supplies; carpeting; and gifts. It also provided a decorating service for homes, schools, apartment buildings, and other residential and commercial buildings.

The Bellefonte Republican, a weekly newspaper, was established on January 6, 1869, by A.B. Hutchinson and W.W. Brown. A few months after its initial publication, R.B. Barger purchased both the *Republican* and another Bellefonte newspaper, the *National*, and consolidated them under the *Republican* title, with the paper also known as *Brown's Bellefonte Republican* during the mid-1870s. Thereafter, the paper changed ownership several more times. However, as of the early 1900s, when this advertising card was distributed to potential subscribers, E.C. Tuten and his son Earl published the *Republican* along with the *Daily News*, another local paper.

✦ Bellefonte ✦ Republican. ✦

THE LEADING PAPER OF CENTRE COUNTY.

CONTAINS MORE HOME NEWS THAN ANY OTHER PAPER PUBLISHED IN THE COUNTY.

The Only Paper in the County that Publishes Telegraphic News.

The Only Paper in the County that has two pages of Pure Reading Matter entirely free from advertisements.

EVERY DEPARTMENT FULL AND COMPLETE.

Now is the Time to Subscribe.

PRICE, $2.00 A YEAR IN ADVANCE.

Address,

REPUBLICAN, Bellefonte, Pa.

[OVER.]

WESLEY. W. TATE

556-4

Given Bellefonte's lack of access to a navigable river, the town's industries primarily relied upon railroads to ship their goods to markets throughout Pennsylvania and beyond, with a dozen or more freight trains passing through Bellefonte each day. One notable short-line railroad, the Bellefonte Central Railroad, the successor to the Buffalo Run, Bellefonte & Bald Eagle Railroad, was a key transportation link for Centre County's iron furnaces. The railroad's scales, shops, and junction were all located at Coleville. On December 1, 1891, the railroad was sold at foreclosure to a group of its Philadelphia bondholders, and reorganized as the Bellefonte Central on May 9, 1892. In 1896, the Bellefonte Central tracks were extended to Pine Grove Mills 20 miles to the southwest, with the line also connecting to State College. The photograph below from the early 1900s shows freight cars parked on sidings along the rail line leading into Bellefonte from Coleville.

On July 24, 1939, Bellefonte received national attention when 27 cars of a 96-car Pennsylvania Railroad freight train wrecked at Central City, two miles outside of town, resulting in a blockage of the heavily traveled route. According to an Associated Press account of the "spectacular wreck," signal towerman Samuel G. Tressler was forced to "leap from a window of his tower . . . to a telephone pole" and then climb down "amid the wreck." One of the derailed train cars crashed into the tower and knocked one corner off the structure. The accident, described by the reporter as one of the "worst wrecks in this district in recent years," was attributed to a broken wheel on the eighth freight car behind the locomotive. Above, a man stands in front of the wrecked train cars. Below, crews work to repair the rails.

Three

FAITH, FAMILY, AND FRIENDS

This early 1900s postcard shows the following downtown Bellefonte churches: Trinity United Methodist Church (top left, corner of West Howard and North Spring Streets), St. John's Roman Catholic Church (top center, East Bishop Street), St. John's Evangelical Lutheran Church (top right, corner of Linn and North Allegheny Streets), United Brethren in Christ Church (center left, corner of West High and North Thomas Streets), St. John's Episcopal Church (bottom center, corner of North Allegheny and Lamb Streets), Evangelical Church (center right, Willowbank Street), First Presbyterian Church (bottom left, corner of Spring and Howard Streets), and St. John's Reformed Church (bottom right, corner of Linn and North Spring Streets).

Shiloh Lutheran Church, midway between Bellefonte and State College, was built in 1868 by a congregation of families whose children attended school nearby. Until 1888, services were held at the church only during the summer owing to the lack of heating. Candles and later oil lamps were used for lighting until electricity was installed in 1938. The church was damaged by lightning in 1921 and repaired.

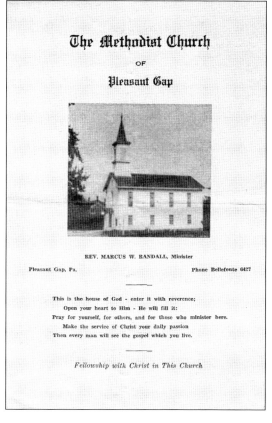

Around 1850, the Pleasant Gap Methodist congregation constructed its first church on present-day South Main Street on land donated by John R. Tate. However, in 1875, the church was accidentally demolished, and a second church was built on the site using some of the lumber from the original building. In the 1970s, the century-old structure shown on this church bulletin was torn down and replaced with a larger, modern church.

The Valley View United Methodist Church, sometimes referred to as the Eckley Church, was built on a hillside overlooking the Nittany Valley a few miles outside of Bellefonte. The church's origins dated to 1896, when a union Sunday school met in the schoolhouse across the street from where the church was eventually constructed and dedicated on August 24, 1902. Later, the church's main entrance was moved from the east side to the north side, and a bell tower and vestibule were added. After the United Brethren church in downtown Bellefonte burned in 1945, the Valley View congregation purchased United Brethren's bell to replace its original bell. At right is an interior view of one of the church's stained-glass windows. The mid-1960s image below shows the church's vacation Bible school class members enjoying lunch. (Both, Earl Houser Jr.)

As evidenced by this photograph, during the early 1900s, adult baptisms, typically held in conjunction with revival meetings, drew large crowds to Bald Eagle Creek at Milesburg, approximately four miles from Bellefonte. Milesburg was founded in the 1790s by Col. Samuel Miles, a Revolutionary War veteran and later mayor of Philadelphia.

Nineteen Hundredth Anniversary

OF

PENTECOST

The Churches of the Pleasant Gap Charge will observe this great New Testament event with PENTECOSTAL Services, Begining Sunday morning June 1. at 11: o clock, Childrens meeting at 2: 30 Pentcostal Services at 7: 30 and each evening during the week at 7:45

SPECIAL WORKERS

Rev. Alice M. Coons, a native and Former missionary of the West Indies, Her message will grip Your Soul. Rev Alma L. Budman, Song leader She sings The gospel Dont Miss One Single Service, Yours For The Fullness of the Blessing

C, A, METZGER, Pastor,

This Pentecostal service announcement from the mid-1920s includes the names of Rev. Alice M. Coons of Endicott, New York, a Pilgrim-Holiness missionary in Barbados, West Indies, and Rev. Alma L. Budman, an ordained Methodist minister, evangelist, and singer. Budman, a resident of Muncy, Pennsylvania, in Lycoming County, was a graduate of the Cleveland Bible Institute and worked in large churches in the western and southern United States.

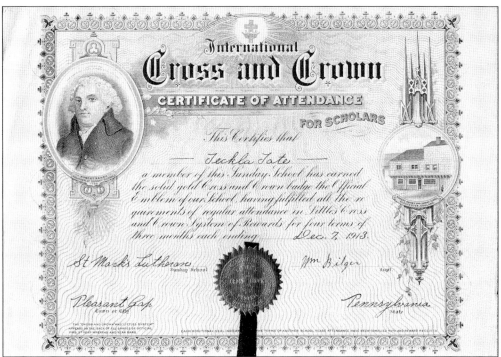

This Cross and Crown certificate shows that Teckla Tate regularly attended Sunday school for four terms of three months ending December 7, 1913. The certificate was issued by the St. Mark's Lutheran Sunday School in Pleasant Gap. St. Mark's was on North Main Street in Pleasant Gap. The first church was built in 1870 and was replaced by a brick structure in 1917.

This announcement was for a free lecture entitled "Why World Powers Are Tottering, The Remedy," by H.H. Dingus, to be given at the Centre County Courthouse on June 8, 1926. The lecture was sponsored by the International Bible Students Association, a group founded in 1872 in Pittsburgh by Charles Taze Russell (1852–1916). Dingus was a Bible scholar who lectured at theaters and other venues in Pennsylvania and elsewhere.

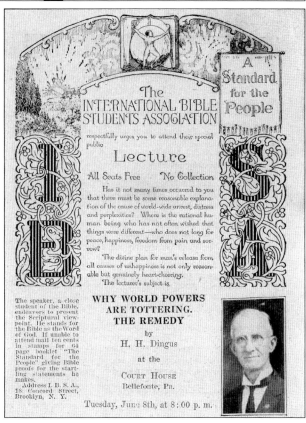

At left, two little girls in their best dresses with ribbons in their hair and holding dolls pose for a portrait at a Bellefonte studio around 1910. The c. 1910s photograph below shows sisters Teckla (left) and Marie Tate on one of Bellefonte's many hilly streets. The sisters maintained close ties throughout their lifetimes. Bellefonte siblings also often worked together in area businesses. For example, the *Democratic Watchman* of November 27, 1914, announced that Lucy Miller had "accepted a position as clerk in Candyland [a downtown candy, ice cream, and soda shop] last Saturday, and yesterday her sister, Miss Jeannette Miller, also went there as a clerk."

In the undated photograph above, Valley View twins William "Billy" Bilger (left) and Nancy (later Burris) smile for the camera. Valley View, described by writer Paul M. Dubbs as "perhaps the longest village in Centre County," stretches along the southern slope of the mountainside "from the hairpin curve above Coleville" to approximately "six miles west of Bellefonte." By 1901, the village consisted of about 18 homes built along both sides of its solitary thoroughfare, Valley View Road. In the photograph below from the early 1900s, Coleville siblings Florence (left) and Elmer Crawford strike an *American Gothic*–style pose with the family's cat for a prop. (Above, Earl Houser Jr.)

It is not known what occasion this group of young Bellefonte area women were celebrating, but their attire suggests that they were marking some type of special event. Owing to the social mores of the time, young women, whether they were sisters, cousins, neighbors, fellow church members, schoolmates, or coworkers, frequently attended social events as a group rather than by themselves.

Outside of school, Bellefonte area youth could earn some money by delivering newspapers, working in downtown stores, or performing other odd jobs. Of course, they also enjoyed some free time to have a little fun, such as striking a pose for the camera, like James Walters Jr. (far right) and two of his Coleville friends did in this undated photograph. (Earl Houser Jr.)

Alvin K. Tate (far left) and his wife, Marguerite, along with another couple and their daughter, pose in front of the Wesley Tate residence at 121 East Bishop Street in downtown Bellefonte. The residence stood directly across from St. John's Catholic Church and across Cherry Alley from the Undine Fire Company firehouse.

The Lowry family reunion was held at the family farmstead on Purdue Mountain. Sherman E. Lowry Sr. married Ulla Bjalme, a daughter of Ivan Bjalme, who came to Bellefonte with his wife and family from Sweden to set up production of safety matches (which could only be lighted when striking a special material on the side of the matchbox) at the Pennsylvania Match Factory.

Family reunions were important annual events in the lives of Bellefonte-area residents. These undated photographs show two gatherings, both possibly Tate family reunions. The Tate family, like many local farm families, had a makeshift picnic area on a wooded lot near their farm outside of Bellefonte. In 1911, the Commonwealth of Pennsylvania purchased the Tate farm along with neighboring farms to construct the Rockview State Correctional Institution.

In the photograph at right from the late 1910s, Coleville friends and coworkers Florence Crawford (left) and Catherine King are having some fun outside the Match Factory. In the undated photograph below, Josephine Yarnell (left) and Betty Lou ? sit on the bumper of an automobile. In the decades after Massachusetts native Anne Rainsford French Bush obtained a steam engineer's license from Washington, DC's municipal authorities in 1900, millions of women joined her in obtaining licenses to drive cars and other vehicles. Bellefonte's female residents were familiar sights on Centre County roads. (Below, Earl Houser Jr.)

In this late 1920s–early 1930s photograph, Pleasant Gap neighbors Edgar "Eddie" Sommers Jr. (left) and Andrew J. Tate Jr. stand in a Main Street backyard. In the 1920s, Edgar's father was a partner in the Sommers and Jodon garage. After dissolving the partnership in the mid-1930s, he started an electrical repair shop at the rear of his property. For many years, he also served as chief electrician at the Grange Encampment and Fair.

This 1920s photograph shows Eddie Longwell (left) and his girlfriend Teckla Tate outdoors at an unidentified location. Tate's mother disapproved of her marrying Longwell owing to his avocation as an aviator, a concern likely shared by other Bellefonte-area parents, given that between August 1918 and September 1927, thirty-four out of the 200 airmail pilots who flew mail perished in plane crashes.

Domesticated animals such as dogs and cats often appeared in photographs of local residents, as illustrated here. As of the early 1960s, the Phoenix Mill in Bellefonte served as the borough's dog pound, with owners required to pay $2 to reclaim their canines. In 1962, Centre County residents owning or harboring unlicensed dogs faced a minimum fine of $5 and costs, 30 days in jail, or both. To make purchasing dog licenses more convenient for owners, Centre County treasurer G.A. Spearly traveled around the county selling licenses at garages and other locations.

In the 1930s photograph at left, Andrew J. Tate Jr. poses in front of the family's barn in Pleasant Gap with his dog Rex. Below, James Walters Jr. poses with his canine companion Snowball. In the early 1960s, enterprising local pet owners could enter their furry friends in the pet show held during the annual Grange Encampment and Fair. In 1961, entrants had a choice of categories including Pets Ridden, Pets Carried, Pets Led, Dogs That Do Tricks, Pets in Homemade Floats, and others. Judges for the 1961 show included Mrs. Sheldon Corl and Mrs. Phil Jodon of State College, Gladys Rearick of Millheim, and Mrs. Car Rudy of Olmstead Falls, Ohio. There were also opportunities for owners to show off their larger animals. For example, in the early 1900s, equine enthusiasts could compete in horse shows and races at the Bellefonte Fairgrounds. (Below, Earl Houser Jr.)

In the 1950s, Winifred Walters gives her daughter, Joanne Walters, a home permanent while the family dog lies nearby. For those who preferred going to a salon, Bellefonte offered a host of options. On Bishop Street, customers could choose from Mary C. Beezer's Beauty Salon at 108 ½ West Bishop or Mary Beradis Beauty Shop at 109 East Bishop, where customers could have their hair permed or cold waved. (Earl Houser Jr.)

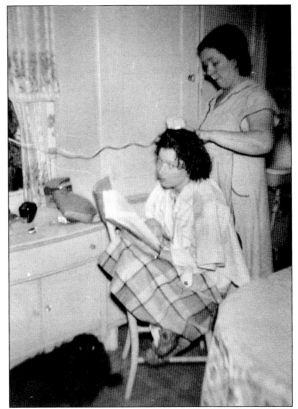

Raising small flocks of chickens was a common practice throughout rural Centre County, including in villages such as Pleasant Gap and Coleville. In this 1930s–1940s photograph, Andrew Tate Sr. is shown with some of the chickens he raised at his home on Main Street in Pleasant Gap. The eggs were used by the families who owned the flocks, with surplus given away or sold from the home or at local markets.

Happy Easter

Let Easter sunshine

Light your way

And make you happy

Throughout the day

Easter was a special holiday for Bellefonte-area residents. Many churches held sunrise services, clubs and organizations held Easter egg hunts, families gathered for home-cooked meals featuring baked ham as the main dish, and adults and children alike dressed up in their new Easter outfits. Other Bellefonte events during the holiday included a Grand Military Ball, held on Easter Monday evening in 1884 in Armory Hall. Above is a 1920s Easter greeting card sent to the Andrew Tate Sr. family in Pleasant Gap. In the 1967 image at left, four-year-old Marsha Ann Tate shows off her stuffed Easter bunny and basket in the front yard of her grandparents' Main Street residence in Pleasant Gap.

Halloween was always a special time, with parties held in homes throughout Bellefonte. In addition, schools and other organizations sponsored parties and costume contests with prizes. Likewise, Bellefonte's community Halloween parade featuring costumed children and other participants was a much-anticipated event. Games and activities such as bobbing for apples and "tame" haunted houses were also familiar features of the season. The children in these early 1970s photographs were attending a party at Earl Houser Sr.'s home outside Bellefonte, with the costumes ranging from the usual ghosts and witches to popular television characters such as H.R. Pufnstuf, Dick Dastardly from *The Wacky Races*, and Buffy from *Family Affair*. (Both, Earl Houser Jr.)

Christmas was always a magical time in Bellefonte. Department stores such as G.C. Murphy Co. and Turner's would welcome shoppers each holiday season. Children had the opportunity to meet Santa and tell him everything that was on their wish list. The activity that was always cherished was setting up the Christmas tree for the season. At left, Earl Houser Jr. is decorating his own silver aluminum tree. Aluminum trees were very popular in the mid-1960s. This tree would be covered with shiny red balls that sparkled from the revolving light wheel that was set up near the tree. The photograph below shows the bottom of a massive pine tree that was set up at the James Walters Sr. residence in Coleville. There was a village under the tree that had a small green wooden fence around it. The tree was adorned with vintage glass ornaments and silver garland icicles that glowed from the strung lights. (Both, Earl Houser Jr.)

Four

SCHOOL DAYS

This undated photograph shows a Centre County schoolteacher and her students standing on the steps of a brick school building. Prior to the flurry of school consolidation in the 1950s, an eclectic array of public schools and private academies was scattered throughout the county. These ranged from one-room wooden schoolhouses where a single teacher taught students of different ages to multiroom brick buildings with modern conveniences.

In his 1915 report to the commonwealth, Centre County school superintendent David O. Etters lamented about the conditions at the county's rural schools: "In many instances too little concern is shown for the condition of the school property. The buildings lack paint, the walls need paper or calcimine and the grounds have run to weeds and briars." However, Etters further noted that Spring Township was erecting a "twin-room [school]house" at Pleasant Gap and that "manual training and domestic science departments of the high school at Bellefonte and at State College are doing excellent work." The report also stated that for the school year ending July 5, 1915, Pennsylvania counted 8,917 male teachers, who earned an average salary of $68.43 per month, and 32,366 female teachers, who earned $50.14 per month.

In the early 1900s, student Leonard Peters sits at his desk reading a book in a Spring Township schoolroom. In 1922, Peters graduated from Spring Township High School in Pleasant Gap. Several schools were built in Pleasant Gap. One, known as the Horntown schoolhouse, was built on the present-day Harrison Road. The building was moved off of the property to allow construction of a second schoolhouse. In addition, a succession of three brick schools were built along the state highway heading over Nittany Mountain (Route 144). Spring Township High School was housed in the brick schools.

After spending his childhood on the family farm in Miles Township, Prof. Cephas Luther (C.L.) Gramley (1852–1935) attended the Clinton Seminary and graduated from Susquehanna University in Selinsgrove, Pennsylvania. After graduation, Gramley returned to Rebersburg in Miles Township, where he taught at the grammar school for 17 years. In 1892, Gramley was named Centre County's superintendent of schools, a position he retained through the 1890s.

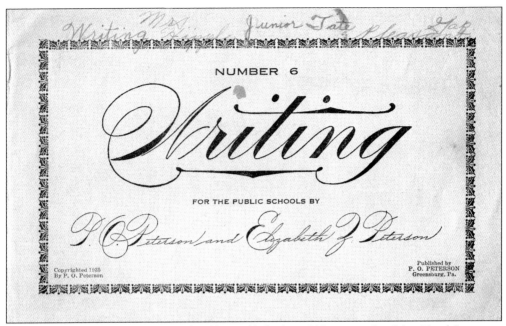

This Peterson and Peterson writing booklet, published in 1935, was used in Miss Hipple's writing class by Pleasant Gap student Andrew Tate Jr. Younger students devoted a substantial amount of their school days to honing their cursive writing and penmanship skills. The series of booklets demonstrated the proper methods for writing the letters of the alphabet.

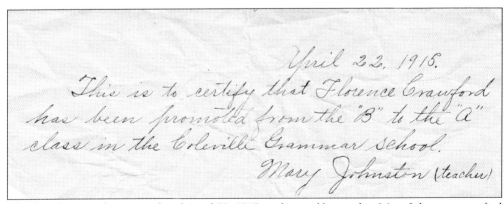

This handwritten document dated April 22, 1915, and signed by teacher Mary Johnston certified that student Florence Crawford was promoted from the B to the A class in the Coleville Grammar School. On March 15, 1912, an unnamed *Democratic Watchman* correspondent put in "a good word for Coleville schools," stating, "it always afforded me much pleasure to find those schools under good pedagogic management and good scholastic deportment."

The two-story brick South Ward School is on East Bishop Street in downtown Bellefonte. The school was built in 1887 by Bellefonte contractor John Robert Cole. Its interior consists of four classrooms on each floor, with a central hallway running between them. As befitting a school, the building's tower included a school bell.

Students who were neither absent nor tardy during the school year were rewarded with a certificate of perfect attendance by the state Department of Public Instruction. In this certificate, student Andrew Tate Jr. was recognized for perfect attendance during the 1934 and 1936–1938 school years.

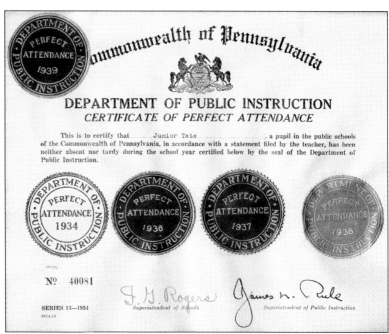

THE TEACHER REQUESTS	MONTH	Days Absent	Times Tardy	Conduct	Reading	Penmanship	Spelling	Arithmetic	Geography	English	History	Health	Music	Drawing	Civics	Signature of Parent or Guardian
That parents keep their children in constant and punctual attendance.	September	0	0	B	C	B		C	C	C	B		B			Mother Houser
That they oversee home studies.	October	2	0	B	C	B		C	C	B	C		B			Miller Houser
That they visit the schools.	November	0	0	B	C	B		C	C	B	C		B			Miller Houser
That they examine and sign this report as often as presented.	December	5	0	C	C	B	D	D	C-	B	C-	D	B			Miller Houser
	January	0	0	C	C	B	B	D+	C	B	D	C				Miller Houser
	February	0	0	C	C	B	C	C-	B	C-	C					Miller Houser
METHOD OF GRADING	March	2	0	C	C	B	a-	C	C	C	C					Miller Houser
A-90 to 100-Excellent	April	0	0	C	C	B	B	B	C	C	C	B				
B-80 to 90-Good	May	1	0	C	C	B	B	C-	C-	D+	D	C-				
C-75 to 80-Medium	June					*Promoted to grade 8*										
D-70 to 75-Doubtful	Average	0	0	C	C	B	C-	C-	C	C	C	C	B			
E-Below 70-Failure																Grace Stover — TEACHER

Report of _Earl Houser_ — 7 Grade
For the year commencing _Sept. 8_ 19_41_, and ending _May 25_ 19_42_

Bellefonte primary and secondary students received report cards such as the one shown here. Course grades, ranging from A (90–100, excellent) to E (below 70, failure) were reported to students and their parents/guardians each month throughout the school year, with an overall average grade assigned at the conclusion of the academic year. Students were required to obtain the signature of their parent or guardian and return the printed card to their teacher. (Both, Earl Houser Jr.)

Individual school photographs, such as these 1933 photographs of Pleasant Gap grammar school student Andrew J. Tate Jr. and his cousin Joanne Walters, were an annual tradition at local schools. A photographer would visit each school, set up a makeshift studio, and take each student's photograph. Copies would typically be distributed to the student's family and friends. Over the years, the pictures also provided cherished snapshots of the student's childhood years. (Below, Earl Houser Jr.)

The four-story brick Bellefonte High School, built in the 1910s, sat on the corner of Allegheny and Linn Streets. On February 13, 1939, a spectacular fire that garnered national notoriety destroyed the stately structure. The blaze, believed to have started near a ventilating fan in the basement, broke out on a school day while 900 students were attending classes. Miraculously, everyone made it out of the building without any fatalities or injuries. This image of the school is from the 1926 *La Belle* yearbook.

The old Bellefonte Armory on the corner of North Spring and West Lamb Streets was built in 1894 by Col. W. Fred Reynolds, nephew of Bellefonte banker and businessman Maj. William F. Reynolds, and transferred to the local National Guard. Following the construction of a new armory, stables, and parade ground on land owned by Harry Lutz southeast of Bellefonte, the downtown property was sold to the Bellefonte school board. Starting in the early 1930s, it was used as a gymnasium, recreation hall, and for other school activities.

In the 1910s photograph at right, Florence Crawford stands in the doorway of Bellefonte High School, while in the 1923 photograph below, Teckla Tate and an unidentified woman (possibly her mother) stand outside the school. In 1924, the 15-member faculty, led by supervising principal Arthur H. Sloop, taught courses that included home economics, music-drama, chemistry, physics, English, history, manual arts, biology, mathematics, French, physical education, Latin, and civics. Sports and other extracurricular activities included the men's relay team, football, track, boys' and girls' basketball, the school newspaper, the Skull and Lantern, and the Red and White Society, whose members served as tour guides for visiting sports teams.

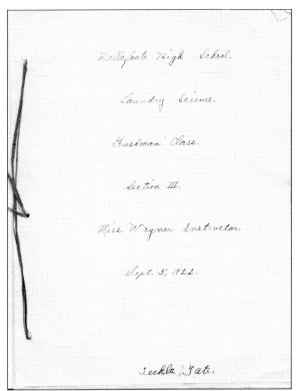

In 1914, Bellefonte Area High School introduced a course in domestic science. The course was financed by the Bellefonte Woman's Club, with one member, Mrs. Olewine, donating over 700 items for use by the class. Pictured is a 1922 laundry science paper submitted by Bellefonte High freshman Teckla Tate to her instructor, Miss Wagner.

La Belle is the annual Bellefonte High School yearbook published by students at the school. The 1926 edition shown here includes portraits of faculty and senior class members as well as a humorous senior class biography that lists each student's name, nickname, favorite expression, "current occupation," and future career goals. For example, Evelyn "Ev" Rogers's favorite expression was "O-Oh G'wan," her occupation was "snoozing in Chem.," and her future aspiration was to be an "authoress."

Following the destruction of Bellefonte High School in February 1939, a new building was constructed on the grounds of the former school at the corner of Allegheny and Linn Streets. The class of 1943 was the first to graduate from the new school, with Dr. Russell Galt, dean of Susquehanna University, delivering the commencement address to the 121 graduates. After the ceremony, the public was invited to view the newly constructed school.

The week of March 29, 1943, was proclaimed Dedication Week for the new Bellefonte High School. The events kicked off on Sunday, March 28, with a religious service in the school auditorium. On Monday, the American Legion performed a patriotic program, also in the auditorium. On Tuesday, a physical education program was given in the gymnasium. Wednesday featured a student's program, and the week-long celebration was capped off on Friday with the official dedication of the school.

DEDICATION
Bellefonte High School

Religious Service
—BY—
THE BELLEFONTE MINISTERIUM
Sunday Evening, March 28, 1943
AUDITORIUM

Program

Opening Remarks...Horace J. Hartranft, President
                                                                        Board of Education
Hymn...Faith of Our Fathers
                              Congregation Standing
The Call to Worship.............................The Reverend C. Nevin Stamm
Selection...The Choir
                    I Will Extol Thee—C. Harold Lowden
Presentation of the Bible..................The Reverend Harry C. Stenger, Jr.
Acceptance of the Bible.......................... Mrs. J. Millard Hartswick,
                                                        Member, Board of Education
Prayer..The Reverend G. E. Householder
Hymn....................................Our God, Our Help In Ages Past
                              Congregation Seated
The Sermon, "Religion and Education"........The Reverend Clarence E. Arnold
Selection...The Choir
              O Lord, How Manifold Are Thy Works—J. Lincoln Hall
Prayer...The Reverend Francis P. Davis
Hymn...My Country, 'Tis of Thee
                              Congregation Standing
The Benediction...............................The Reverend H. Halbert Jacobs
             Choir Director...............................Mrs. J. Ernest Martin
             Pianist...Mrs. Paul S. Beaver
     The Choir consists of representatives of the Bellefonte Church Choirs

Further Schedule of Events For Dedication Week

Monday, March 29—Patriotic Program, American Legion................Auditorium
Tuesday, March 30—Physical Education Program...........................Gymnasium
Wednesday, March 31—Student's Program.....................................Auditorium
Thursday, April 1—Dedication..Auditorium
            All programs begin at 7:45 P. M.

The celebrations surrounding the construction of a new high school were overshadowed by World War II, with numerous students leaving their studies to enlist in the armed forces. This undated photograph is of a war-era class at Bellefonte. Students who remained on the home front contributed to the war effort by selling war bonds and through other activities.

Pictured is the December 7, 1942, issue of the *Red & White News*, Bellefonte High School's student newspaper. In 1921, the paper began as a monthly publication entitled the *Racket*, but the name was changed at a later date. In addition to publishing school-related news, the paper also solicited advertising from local merchants.

This c. 1940s photograph may be of the graduating class of Spring Township High School in Pleasant Gap, since it is smaller than Bellefonte High classes shown in other photographs in this chapter. In the early to mid-1940s, Spring Township High School was a two-year institution, with students transferring to Bellefonte for their junior and senior years following their "graduation" (after the tenth grade) from Spring Township.

With 55 students, Bellefonte High School's graduating class of 1922 was the largest to date. The commencement ceremony capped a weeklong series of events including a baccalaureate sermon delivered by Rev. David E. Evans at the Presbyterian church downtown; a performance of *The Enchanted Garden*, a "musical phantasy," by the grade school pupils; a high school glee club play, *When Reuben Comes to Town*; and more. The commencement speaker was Dr. Emory Hunt, president of Bucknell University. Pictured here is a 1922 commencement announcement from Irene Maud Stover.

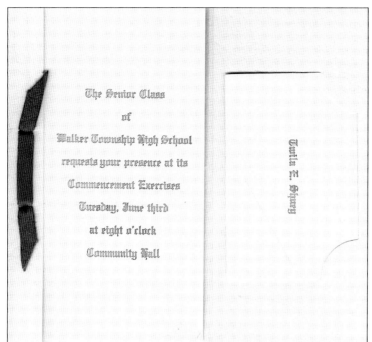

This commencement announcement is from Twila E. Shuey, a member of the 1930 senior class at Walker Township High School in Hublersburg, approximately 16 miles north of Bellefonte. In 1957, as part of a countywide consolidation of public schools, Walker Township High closed, and students transferred to Bellefonte Area High School. An elementary school continued to operate in the village.

This 1973–1974 Pleasant Gap Elementary School class photograph shows fourth-grade students with their teacher, Dorothy Dobelbower. The school, on South Main Street, had been the site of Spring Township High School until the 1940s. Due to space constraints, kindergarten classes were held across the street on the bottom floor of the Pleasant Gap United Methodist Church's fellowship hall.

Five

THE GREATEST GENERATION

Bellefonte residents helped fill the ranks of troops in the Civil War, Spanish-American War, World War I, and other conflicts over the years. The Bellefonte American Legion Post 33 was named in memory of Privates Edward B. Brooks and Charles F. Doll, the first two members of Troop L, Bellefonte, to be killed in World War I. This early 1900s photograph shows a Bellefonte resident in uniform.

Pleasant Gap resident Andrew J. Tate Jr., the son of Andrew and Florence Tate, was one of the Bellefonte High School students who left school to join the armed forces as soon as he reached enlistment age. During his 22-month tour of duty, Private First Class Tate served in England, France, Belgium, and Germany, participating in the Normandy invasion, the Battle of the Bulge, and several other historic military engagements. He was awarded five Bronze Stars and the Good Conduct Medal while serving with the 9th Air Force.

In this early 1950s photograph, Earl Houser Sr., dressed in his military uniform, stands with his mother, Gertrude Houser, in the Houser family's backyard in Valley View. Houser, also a Bellefonte High School graduate, was a veteran of the Korean Conflict. Centre County military casualties included 7 in Korea and 19 in Vietnam. (Earl Houser Jr.)

Lucinda Hall (1873–1963) was a Bald Eagle Valley resident and ardent supporter of Bellefonte's military personnel. She unfailingly walked the several miles from her home to the Bellefonte train station to salute departing Centre County service members as they left their hometown to fight in World War II and later in Korea.

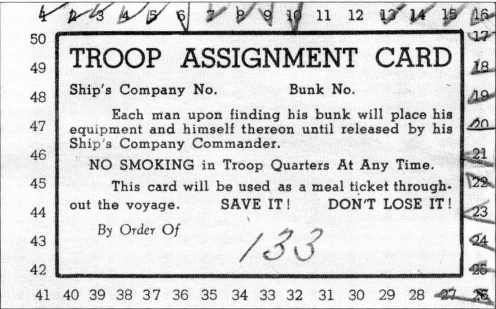

During World War I, several decades prior to the patriotic endeavors of Lucinda Hall, the *Democratic Watchman* shared a request from the US Council of National Defense asking community members to assemble at registration sites and sing "national and patriotic songs . . . just before the noon hour, late in the afternoon and again in the evening." However, once the fanfare was over, soldiers faced the realities of military life. One indispensable item for World War II soldiers was the Troop Assignment Card, which also served as their meal ticket as they journeyed by sea to the war zones.

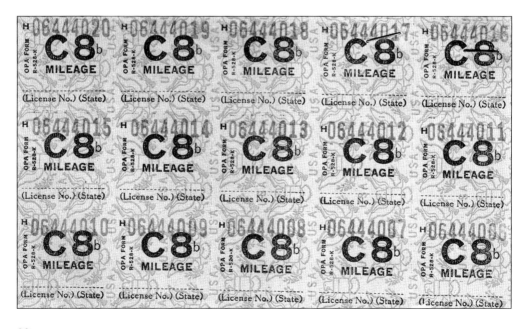

During World War II, the rationing of gas and other commodities was a fact of life for Bellefonte residents. Pictured here are a ration card and coupons issued by the War Price & Rationing Board, which maintained an office on West High Street in downtown Bellefonte. Food rationing began in the spring of 1942, followed by rubber and gasoline rationing in December of the same year. Windshield stickers were issued, with "A" stickers entitling drivers to four gallons of gas per week; "B" for business owners, who were allotted eight gallons; "C" for those in professional occupations; "M" for motorcycles; and "T" for truck drivers. (Both, Earl Houser Jr.)

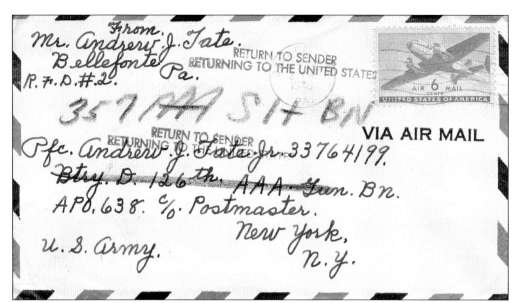

In the era before email, texting, and social media, soldiers and their families had to rely on traditional mail to exchange news. During World War II, letters sent by soldiers overseas to their loved ones were screened by censors, who redacted selected portions of letters that they believed could reveal troop movements or other potentially damaging information related to the Allied cause. This letter was returned for a more auspicious reason: the soldier was returning home to Bellefonte.

"Hello Son"   Bellefonte, Pa,
                                          Nov. 19-45
        How is our young man today? We are
well, hope you are in the best of health. We
had a wet day here. It rained pretty smart
all day. I was picking off bad eggs today, to
marrow we will go over to Spring Creek and
take some more eggs. Today was off from work
this after noon, he went over to Lewistown for
Lois, she was down in Florida with her Husband, but it cost to much for her to stay
down there. She was down about a month.
Deforest Moyer is home, and discharged from
the army. David Pahlgreen who is a fish warden
from Philipsburg, said his son is a guard over
Hess, and some of those fellows at Nuremburg.
He don't expeck to get home until next year
some time. He was only over the pond a little
while before the war quit. He went in the army
at 18 and was not on this side very long, about like
you. Arthur Brodford is back to the hatchery.
You remember of him, he works in the Labriatory
and before he went to the army he used to board
at Jim Parks. Sheldon Shuey started to work
at White rock today. He is filling bags in the
pulverizeing plant. Mother done the washing today, and is drying the clothes on the porch and
down in the cellar. I washed the supper dishes
tonight and mother dried them. We decided to
put you on K.P. when you get home. Paul Poorman
had tough luck already at the Titon. You can
read the piece about him. Well this is Tuesday
morning Nov. 20th. and it is not raining today.
I am going to iron after I get my other work
done up. Hope we get some good news from you
today. The 25th of Oct was my latest letter.
Be careful and we wish you the best of luck.
We hope to see you before long. Chuck
Chuck is in this letter I think. The picture of the
Will say so long. With lots of love + a kiss X X X X
Dad + Mother. Write when you can. Be good.

This 1946 Bellefonte High class photograph provides a contrast to earlier class photos, especially the first row of students, with a group of six in military uniforms. Barring World War II, most, if not all, of these uniformed individuals would have graduated two years earlier. However, upon finishing their tours of duty, they returned to high school to complete their educations.

In 1947, Bellefonte High's World War II veterans returned to their alma mater for this photograph. Some of them continued their education at Penn State and other colleges via the Servicemen's Readjustment Act of 1944 (the GI Bill), while others found employment in the local area and elsewhere.

Six

FISHERMAN'S PARADISE

Fed by limestone springs, the Spring Creek waterway that passes through downtown Bellefonte and its tributaries have the distinction of being some of the best trout streams in the United States. The Bellefonte area's three fish hatcheries and its natural trout stream habitats have played a prominent role in Centre County's history. This is a June 1934 photograph of hatchery worker Andrew Tate Sr. standing on a road used to feed and access the growing freshwater fish, mainly trout.

Bellefonte Hatchery, Penna. State Fi
Copyright 1908 by R

Plans for Centre County's first fish hatchery began in 1903, when W.E. Meehan, Pennsylvania's commissioner of fisheries, selected a "site near Bellefonte . . . to replace a dilapidated hatchery at Allentown." In the 1903–1904 *Report of the Department of Fisheries of the Commonwealth of Pennsylvania*, Meehan explained that he selected the site because the "citizens of Centre County presented a large tract of land" for the proposed hatchery. Nevertheless, construction of the new

hatchery—approximately three miles from Bellefonte and a half mile outside Pleasant Gap—was initially delayed owing to the lack of a "dwelling house or barn" on the property. Moreover, the site's adjoining property owner held the water rights to the spring that had been designated as the hatchery's water source. This is a 1908 photograph of the Pleasant Gap Hatchery. (Courtesy of the Library of Congress.)

The Commonwealth of Pennsylvania entered into a 99-year lease at $50 a year to obtain the right to use water from Logan Branch Run, which ran parallel to the hatchery site. The stream alone could provide the hatchery with an additional 8,000 gallons of water per minute, thereby giving the facility an ample supply. Also visible in this February 1942 photograph are a group of large aerators used to help provide the young fish in the hatchery with the oxygen they needed. (Photograph by Ward Sampsell.)

Pleasant Gap Fish Hatchery employees Andrew J. Tate Sr. (left) and Guy Moyer stand in front of the hatch house at the facility. The Tate family farm was next door to the hatchery, and Andrew, who had no desire to farm, sought employment at the facility as soon as he came of age.

Above, Andrew Tate Sr. (left) and a fish culturist work in the hatch house at the Pleasant Gap Fish Hatchery. Fish farming, like its livestock counterpart, requires caring for aquatic life around the clock. As of 1922, fish culturists worked nine hours per day (eight hours on Saturday), six days per week, with no overtime pay. Employees were also required to work every other Sunday and were paid a $90 per month salary. At right, another fish culturist works in the hatch house at Pleasant Gap hatchery.

Pleasant Gap Fish Hatchery employee John Weaver stands on the back of a hatchery truck loaded with buckets and pans used to feed the young fish in the hatchery's holding ponds. A driver would slowly drive the truck on the dirt roads running between the long narrow ponds while the employee on the back would throw the feed into the ponds.

In August 1950, Andrew Tate Sr. stands in the middle of the holding ponds at the Pleasant Gap Fish Hatchery, feeding fish. Hatchery workers had to navigate narrow concrete paths (typically the sides of holding ponds) while carrying feed buckets and other equipment. This required excellent balance and could be a perilous exercise, especially during the winter. (Photograph by Calvin Conklin.)

In 1933–1934, the state constructed the Bellefonte State Fish Hatchery, consisting of raceways, display pools, and a hatcher building. On May 25, 1934, a model trout farm and stream improvement project hailed as the first of its kind in the United States was unveiled at the newly constructed hatchery. The one-mile-long fishing area on Spring Creek adjacent to the hatchery became known as "Fisherman's Paradise." Guests at the opening ceremony included Pennsylvania governor Gifford Pinchot and well-known individuals from the fields of fly fishing, plug casting, fly tying, stream improvement, and related specialties. These luminaries were joined by hundreds of local and out-of-town fishermen who were eager to test their angling skills in the reinvigorated waterway, which now included boulder deflectors and winter holes for trout. The hatchery's 42 permanent ponds teemed with over 260,000 juvenile brook and brown trout, which would be transported by train throughout the state upon reaching maturity. The 1942 photograph above shows the visitors center/offices at Fisherman's Paradise. The postcard below shows fishermen enjoying Fisherman's Paradise. (Above, photograph by Ward Sampsell.)

This photograph, taken June 15, 1960, shows three of the Pleasant Gap Fish Hatchery's veteran employees: (from left to right) G.E. Moyer, aged 62, a 40-year employee; G.B. Kerstetter, aged 61; and Andrew J. Tate Sr., aged 58 and a 37-year employee at the hatchery. (Photograph by Johnny Nicklas, courtesy of the Pennsylvania Fish Commission.)

Of course the favorite pastime of fish hatchery employees was fishing, a sport shared by many other individuals in other professions as well, as attested by the large numbers of anglers and other visitors to Fisherman's Paradise and to the prime fishing waters in the Bellefonte area. In this photograph, Andrew J. Tate Sr. shows off one of the trout he caught on Logan Branch.

Seven

HOMETOWN FUN

From high school homecoming, Fourth of July, and Halloween parades to carnivals and festivals, along with countless other special occasions, Bellefonte's community celebrations are memorable events, often drawing thousands of participants and spectators alike. In this undated photograph, the Undine Fire Company's parade unit is shown marching in a parade.

Impressed by the impact YMCAs were having on other communities throughout the United States and elsewhere, former Civil War general and Bellefonte-based attorney James Beaver spearheaded efforts to form both the Pennsylvania and Bellefonte chapters of the YMCA. The Bellefonte YMCA was established on October 19, 1869, making it only the third YMCA chartered in the state, with Beaver serving as the first chief volunteer officer of the facility. Bellefonte's YMCA facilities included a large indoor swimming pool, shown below in 1912. The first Bellefonte High School basketball game was played in the YMCA gymnasium on January 29, 1909, against Lock Haven. Bellefonte won 58-4. (Below, courtesy of the Library of Congress.)

Petrikin Hall on West High Street was built in 1901–1902 for the Women's Christian Temperance Union (WCTU). The building's ground floor consisted of two large rooms—one occupied by the WCTU and the other by the public library. It also included a large hallway leading to an auditorium that could seat from 600 to 800 people, together with a stage that could accommodate 150. The second and third floors held six apartments. The WCTU auditorium was later known as the Scenic Theatre, a venue for live performances and "better-class photoplays," as noted in a 1922 *Democratic Watchman* ad.

Bellefonte residents participated in a variety of bands and other musical groups. One of these was the Titan Chorus, comprised of Titan Metal employees. The choir was formed on July 24, 1942, with Lenore Martin serving as its director and voice teacher and J.Y. Sieg as business manager. The group performed at various events in Bellefonte and in surrounding communities. (Courtesy of the Centre County Library & Historical Museum.)

Scenic Theatre

WHERE THE BETTER CLASS PHOTOPLAYS ARE SHOWN
PROGRAM FOR THE WEEK OF MAY 24, 1926.

GLORIA SWANSON
in "THE UNTAMED LADY"
Tuesday, Wednesday, May 25, 26

Bellefonte residents enjoyed live and later filmed entertainment at several downtown theaters. These included the Garman Opera House, built in 1887 as an opera house and later converted to a movie theater, and the adjacent State Theater, built in 1890. In its heyday, the State hosted many vaudeville and other performers, including the comedy duo of George Burns and Gracie Allen and famed escape artist Harry Houdini. Pictured is a 1926 pamphlet listing coming events at the Scenic Theatre, located on the first floor of Petrikin Hall, and the nearby Moose Theatre. In February 1926, a *Democratic Watchman* correspondent effusively praised another movie shown at the Scenic: "Every person who flocked to the Scenic last week to see *The Merry Widow*, and hundreds of people were there, could not fail but be impressed with the high class of pictures being shown at the popular place of amusement." The writer also complimented Bernice Crouse for "the splendid music produced . . . [on] the theater's big pipe organ."

SCENIC THEATRE
BELLEFONTE, PA.

EACH EVENING AT 6:30 P. M.
EXCEPT SATURDAY AT 6:15 P. M.

Matinees Discontinued for the Summer

PROGRAM

Monday, May 24—Carl Laemmle presents
REGINALD DENNY
In a merry tale of laughs and thrills
"I'LL SHOW YOU THE TOWN"
He is beset by a prim widow madly infatuated with him. Then a friend's wealthy ward is sent to him for guardianship. Then, to add to his troubles, a former sweetheart—now married—breezes in without her husband.
Pathe News   Aesop's Fables
Single Variety Reel, "Canary Island"

Tuesday and Wednesday, May 25 and 26—
A Paramount Picture
GLORIA SWANSON
In a deluxe society love comedy
"THE UNTAMED LADY"
With a special cast, including
Lawrence Gray & Joseph Smiley
Adapted from a story by Fannie Hurst
A luxurious society comedy-romance with dramatic trimmings. The heroine, a girl with twenty millions and an ungovernable temper, falls in love with a man who tries to break her, but he only succeeds when, after he is injured, his weakness conquers where his strength had failed.
Mack Sennett Laugh Riot, "Wandering Papas"

Scenic Theatre   **Program Continued**

Thursday, May 27—
"FLAMES"
With a brilliant cast, including
VIRGINIA VALLI
Eugene O'Brien & Jean Hersholt
A thrilling, spectacular drama of amazing action and deep heart interest and appeal.
Pathe News   Pathe Review

Friday, May 28—Universal presents
JACK HOXIE
In his latest production
"THE DEMON"
A screen drama of adventure in the great outdoors—a story that will give new shivers to your spine, new thrills to your senses, new shocks to your heart. Rattling action from the opening to the closing scene.
Dorothy Phillips in first chapter of "Bar C Mystery"

Saturday, May 29—First National presents
"FIFTH AVENUE"
A story of Metropolitan life, with
MARGUERITE DE LA MOTTE
A smashing picturization of the famous Saturday Evening Post story by Arthur Stringer—a vivid, realistic, colorful and human story of the highways and byways of Metropolitan life. A story of Fifth Avenue—its splendor and its sophistry—its sophistication and its sham — put into a drama that has been filmed on the actual scenes.
Fox first run two reel Comedy, "Eight Cylinder Bull"

Program Subject to Change at Discretion of Management

In addition to filmed entertainment, Bellefonte residents could view live theatrical performances at the Moose Theatre (renamed the State Theatre in 1928). At the time, it was Bellefonte's largest theater, with 740 seats in the orchestra section and 150 in the balcony. The Moose hosted touring companies such as the Graham Stock Company, which presented "complete productions of recent Broadway plays."

The Moose Theatre also catered to boxing and wrestling aficionados, periodically hosting matches at the building. The boxers and wrestlers were a mix of local and out-of-town talent. This undated ad from the *Democratic Watchman* announces the card for an upcoming boxing match at the site sponsored by the Bellefonte Amusement Association.

Capt. JOHN WARD, S. S. N. Y's.

COPYRIGHTED BY GOODWIN & CO. 1887.

GOODWIN & CO. New York.

Baseball Hall of Fame inductee and lawyer John Montgomery Ward was born in Bellefonte in 1860. An exceptional student, Ward was attending Penn State by the age of 13, but following the death of his parents, he was forced to quit college and find a job. Thereafter, he discovered the sport of baseball. After playing on semipro teams for several years, Ward joined the National League's Providence Grays in 1878 as a pitcher. Ward also played outfield, shortstop, and second base during his career. In addition, he served as the team's player-manager intermittently during seven seasons. During the offseason, he earned a law degree from Columbia in 1885, followed by a political science degree in 1886. Ward initiated the first-ever baseball players' union in 1885 and continued to practice law following his retirement from baseball at the age of 34. (Both, courtesy of the Library of Congress.)

In 1894, the Central Railroad of Pennsylvania purchased land approximately eight miles outside of Bellefonte and constructed Hecla Park. The park included a wooded picnic area, a large dam for boating and bathing, and a large, covered dance pavilion (later a skating rink). Over time, a large swimming pool, children's playground, Ferris wheel, merry-go-round, and other amenities were added. The park's formal opening was August 9, 1894, when the Logan Steam Fire Engine Company of Bellefonte was scheduled to hold its annual picnic at the site. The park remained one of Centre County's most popular parks into the mid-20th century. The 1949 photograph above shows (from left to right) Ada Hicks, Vesta Barnes, and Alice Muirhead canoeing on Hecla Park's lake. Below, young women sit alongside Hecla Park's boating area. (Above, Earl Houser Jr.)

Bellefonte residents have had a long-standing affection for their motor vehicles. For generations, "lapping the block," or driving cars around the block, which included going past the Diamond, was a Friday night ritual for young adults. In fact, many married couples first met while lapping the block. The activity was outlawed by the borough council in the late 1970s. In the undated photograph at left, Earl Houser Sr. sits on his motorcycle, while below, the Walters family's dog sits in the driver's seat of the car, awaiting a road trip. (Both, Earl Houser Jr.)

This 1895 photograph shows the First National Bank building and neighboring Crider Exchange building on North Allegheny Street festooned with bunting to celebrate Bellefonte's centennial. The photograph also provides a glimpse of a group of Bellefonte residents standing in front of the buildings. After the First National Bank was destroyed by fire in 1888, the building was rebuilt in 1889 along with the Crider Exchange. (Courtesy of the Pennsylvania State University Libraries.)

Bellefonte Brothers of the Brush

CELEBRATING THE SESQUICENTENNIAL
OF BELLEFONTE

This is to certify that I, *Andrew J. Tate Jr.* being a good civic-minded citizen or resident of Bellefonte area, agreed to grow a moustache, full beard, goat-tee or side-burns as a part of the Bellefonte Sesquicentennial Celebration to be held from August 12th to August 18th, this year, 1956 A. D., and is a member in good standing.

Bellefonte Sesquicentennial Beard Committee

Button Issue ☐

In conjunction with Bellefonte's sesquicentennial celebration during the summer of 1956, local men joined the Bellefonte Brothers of the Brush. The club's initiation required the growing of a "moustache, full beard, goat-tee or side-burns" for the August 12–18 celebration.

During Bellefonte's 1956 sesquicentennial celebration, merchants distributed wooden coins such as the "five wooden nickels" pictured here. The coins could be used to purchase goods at any participating business or be redeemed for their face value at either Bellefonte bank on or before August 15, 1956. In addition, souvenir plates featuring the images of Bellefonte's governors along with other items were sold. A writer for the *Tyrone Daily Herald* lauded Bellefonte's celebration: "There certainly was no lack of spontaneous 'good times' and impressive demonstrations. Parades, contests of all sorts, and an historical pageant turned the town into a gala festival for a week." The correspondent was especially enthralled with the pageant *Bellefonte Through the Years*.

Eight

THE BELLEFONTE BANJO BAND

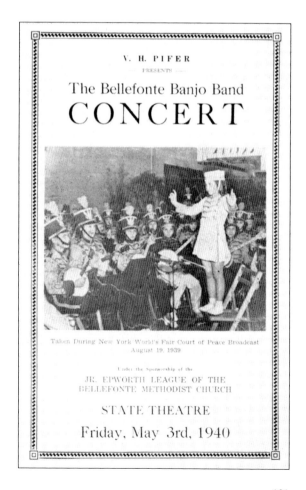

V. H. PIFER

PRESENTS

The Bellefonte Banjo Band
CONCERT

Taken During New York World's Fair Court of Peace Broadcast
August 19, 1939

Under the Sponsorship of the

JR. EPWORTH LEAGUE OF THE
BELLEFONTE METHODIST CHURCH

STATE THEATRE

Friday, May 3rd, 1940

In 1933, in the depths of the Great Depression, Linn Street resident and banjo teacher Victor H. Pifer formed the Bellefonte Banjo Band, which started out with eight players. Over the next nine years, the band would develop into a nationally known group comprised of up to 100 or more musicians at any one time.

The Bellefonte Banjo Band's membership was made up of young men and women who were also Pifer's music students. In addition to giving lessons in Bellefonte, Pifer traveled to communities throughout central Pennsylvania, including Milesburg, Beech Creek, Belleville, Blanchard, Centre Hall, and Lock Haven, giving lessons in a different town each day. For a time, he also

gave lessons in Snow Shoe and Clarence as well. Although the banjo was the band's predominant instrument, the guitar, piano, bass, bells, and other instruments also joined in performances. The State Theatre in downtown Bellefonte served as the band's regular indoor concert venue, and that is where this undated photograph of the band was taken.

This 1930s photograph of the Bellefonte Banjo Band provides a more detailed view of the band members and their instruments. As shown, band members ranged in age from nine or so years old through their teenage years and even older. Parents of various band members acted as chaperones when the band traveled to out-of-town events.

In this late 1930s photograph, first tenor banjo player Andrew J. Tate Jr. stands in the yard of his family's Main Street home wearing his banjo band uniform. The band, an independent organization, did not solicit contributions; instead, its revenue was derived from concerts, parade fees, festivals, and other appearances. Uniforms, music, supplies, and travel expenses were paid for out of the band treasury.

The Bellefonte Banjo Band's monthly newsletter, the *Music Box*, kept members and their families informed about the band's activities and its members. The typewritten, typically one-page, mimeographed publication was edited by the band's director, Vic Pifer. The newsletters show the band's busy schedule during the mid- to late 1930s. For example, in the August 1935 edition, Pifer lists the band's 13 performances during the year to date; he also notes that "nine engagements were turned down because of the band being already engage on date wanted." The summer 1935 newsletters repeatedly advertised the band's "Big Picnic" to be held in September at Hecla Park. In addition to a potluck dinner, the main band joined with the junior bands from Bellefonte, Clarence, and Lock Haven for a joint performance.

Festival Edition "The Music Box" August, 1935

THANK YOU!
The Bellefonte Banjo Band takes this means to express appreciation to all those who helped in such a splendid way in making it's festival a success. The band hopes it may some day have the privilege of returning the favor.

$30.36 CLEAR
That is a lot of money and it shows what a hard working and co-operating organization can do. The Banjo Band Festival of August 3rd was a smashing success. The crowd was on the job-the full band on the job and parents and friends helped in a big way. Full detail of the festival is shown on page two of the MUSIC BOX.

LETTERS SENT OUT
Mrs. Guy Housel sent out appreciation letters to those firms who contributed in any way to the festival work. Mrs. Housel is the band secretary and is kept very busy this summer with the banjo band's many activities.

THIS FAR--
the banjo band has played at the following engagements:
1. Howard
2. Colevills
3. Bush Addition
4. V.F.W.-Bellefonte
5. Union Picnic-Hecla Park
6. Pleasant Gap
7. P.O.S.of A.-Bellefonte
8. "
9. Valley View
10. Blossburg
11. Howard
12. B.B.B. Festival-Bellefonte
13. Scotia Picnic- Scotia
(others pending)
nine engagements were turned down because of the band being already engaged on date wanted.

THE NEXT BAND CONTEST-
will be in (Minneapolis(1936) But in 1937 it will be in Detroit, Mich., and the band is hoping to have it's treasure well supplied by that time so that it can attend and bring home the Bacon in the form of a prize cup. The Banjo Band from Berwik, Pa. that played in the contest this year failed to win, although they did have a good band.

CHARLES SMITH RESIGNS--
Dear Members of the Bellefonte Banjo Band: It is with deep regret that I hereby resign from the office of president due to the inability to participate in any of your actions because of my joining the Hecla Park dance Orchestra.-Yours very truly, --Charles Smith

It is with regret that we received the above note. Mr. Smith has been a very efficient officer who worked hard before and during his term of office. We of the banjo band wish him much success in his future endeavors.

THE BIG PICNIC--
has been planned for the 1st or 8th of September at Hecla Park. This will be the big day for all who play or study the fretted instruments in and near this section of the state. Many are planning on attending from Lock Haven, Beech Creek, Mill Hall, Clarence, Snow Shoe and all are coming with the idea of having one grand time. There will be races, horse shoe and other events. All will enjoy a potluck dinner. One of the big attractions will be the playing of the banjo band augmented by the junior bands on Bellefonte, Clarence and Lock Haven. This should make a banjo band of around 75 players. The exact date will be announced in plenty of time for all to make arrangements to go.

NEW BAND PRESIDENT--
Mr. Joseph Kustenbauter was appointed as the new band president at the business meeting Aug. 5th Joe, as we all know, is a hard working member and will be well liked in his new office. He ran a close second in the annual election some time ago for the General Managership now held by Capt. A.T.Houck.

NEW ADDITION-WELCOME!
Miss Ellen Dottig has been appearing with the banjo band glee club recently and now has an official sweater and is considered a member and we will guess that she will be an active one.

December, 1935   Christmas Edition--

CHRISTMAS CAROL SING
On Wed. night, Dec 23rd, the Bellefonte Banjo Band invites everyone to play and sing carols. The band will form about 9 o'clock on the diamond or the court house steps and it is hoped that several hundred singers will join in the singing. In addition to several marches, the band will play the following songs: Joy To The World, Silent Night, Jingle Bells and Santa Claus Is Coming To Town.

It seems that several years ago carols were sung on the streets of Bellefonte, but since that time it has been sadly neglected. It is proper that the banjo band, Bellefonte's largest musical organization, should sponsor the event.

The 125 pce. band, 30 other fretted instrument players from this school will be augmented by others, harmonica and brass instrument players from Bellefonte and nearby towns. All are invited.

Local newspapers are interested and Mrs. Krader has voiced her approval. The Banjo Band has a habit of doing things in a big way---Lets make this carol sing the BEST YET.

NEW PUPILS AT CLARENCE
People are very much interested in music at Clarence, Pa. Eight weeks ago we started 20 new pupils there and the following are the names of who started two weeks past: Max Reese, William Weislagle Maxine and Calvin Stark, Robert Morgan, and Gaylon Maning. Vera Lewis joined a week before the last class. Best wishes from the MUSIC BOX. Your instructor has just presented the Clarence School with 35 new community song books to be used in Miss Meek's room.

NEWS WILL-------
Gerald Nolen, a promising young banjo player, has been in the Centre County Hospital because of injuries received while sled riding. His mother reports that he will soon be allowed to return to his home. Best wishes from THE MUSIC BOX, Gerald.-------- Several brass instrument players augmented the banjo band at a recent rehearsal to very good advantage. As new members fights out is worked into pretty good shape now and work will soon begin on the convention contest March "Connecticut".--- The Biggest guitar in the world is now a feature of the banjo band and Haw. orchestra. It is as large and is played like a double bass. Ethel is the player.------ Ivy recently played piano in a program over WRAK, Williamsport. The band is due to play there this winter.----

THANK YOU!
for your interest in and support of the Music Box and it's writer this past year. It has been a great pleasure and privilege to serve you and work with you. This writer assures you that he will do his very best to help you this coming year, which, by the way, is mainly to look like a very interesting and musical one. With items or news etc, we are ready with many new events already scheduled for you. The Best Wishes and THANK YOU!
V. H. P.

WE CLOSE THIS MUSIC BOX FOR ANOTHER YEAR
WITH THE HOPE IT HAS BROUGHT YOU WORDS OF GOOD CHEER
LET US START '37 WITH ALL RECORDS MET
AND ALL PLAY TOGETHER AS BAND PLAYERS DO.

NEW YORK WORLD'S FAIR 1939

incorporated

SPECIAL WEEK-END

SOUVENIR

ATTACHED COUPON GOOD ONLY ON

SATURDAY or SUNDAY

PRESIDENT

N⁰ _280515_

TREASURER

Many of the banjo band members (or their families) rarely, if ever, ventured beyond central Pennsylvania, so performing in front of an international audience at the 1939 World's Fair in New York City was a once-in-a-lifetime opportunity. Pictured is a special weekend souvenir train ticket issued by the Pennsylvania Railroad to a band member who departed from Bellefonte on their journey to New York City. Other members of the band drove by automobile to Lewistown and boarded the train there. The back of the ticket (below) is stamped with the departure date of August 19, 1939. In addition to their personal belongings, band members also traveled with their instruments, music, and uniforms.

The band's World's Fair itinerary for August 19 and 20, 1939, shows a full schedule for members. The day after performing at the World's Fair Court of Peace broadcast, the band toured the city by bus, then enjoyed a four-hour boat ride, followed by a visit to the broadcast studios at Rockefeller Center in Midtown Manhattan. It concluded, "Bring your camera, take notes, etc. MAKE THE MOST OF IT."

BELLEFONTE BANJO BAND SCHEDULE OF EVENTS PROGRAM-AT FAIR

August 19th, 20th, 1939

11:30 PM Leave Bellefonte by Auto Friday Aug. 18th
1:27 AM   "   Lewistown on train (special coach for girls, coach for boys) Saturday Aug. 19th
7:30 AM(E.S.T.) Arrive Pennsy Station N.Y.C. Wash up-Have Breakfast at Rest. Across Street
8:30 Leave Pennsy Station for Fair (10¢)
9:00 Be met at Fair Gate by Mrs. Bright and police escort to go directly to General Motors Exhibit
10:00 Other Transportation Buildings
11:30 Lunch at nearby stands
12:00 To Pennsylvania Building for uniform changing
1:00 Court Of Peace Concert
2:00 Parade of amusement Area and Childs World
3:00 Picture taken at G.M. Bldg.
3:45 Concert at Goodrich Show
4:00 Goodrich Show in honor of banjo band
5:00 Take off uniforms at Penna. Bldg.
6:00 Dinner at nearby stands
7:00 Free two hours to enjoy any of Fair grounds and Amusement
9:00 Return to Penna. Bldg., to view beautiful fountain display.
10:00 Leave grounds for Hotel Park Central in N.Y.C. (10¢)
12:00 Midnight "ALL IN Bed"

SUNDAY--AUGUST 20th

7:30 All up, breakfast, swim in hotel pool.
9:15 EVERYONE goes to Sunday School in ... (... ... to church)
10:30 Back to rooms, wash up, check out of hotel and have lunch
11:45 Get aboard bus for city tour which ends at steamboat dock at
2:00 P.M. Get on Steamer for four hour boat ride.
6:00 Get aboard cross town busses(5¢) Arrive at hotel, wash up, walk to 6th Ave. & 50th St. Automat for evening meal, then across street to Rockefeller Development to visit roof and broadcasting studios.
10:00 leave to walk to Pennsy Station passing through Times Sq. and Great White Way at night.
11:00 or 10:00 Eastern Standard Time arrive at Station to await our train for home at 11:40. Arrive Lewistown 4:15 AM Monday.

NOTES

Each band member must have dimes and nickels ready for fares
All meals to be paid for by individual
Bathing suits and towels will be furnished by hotel
Tips to hotel attendants to be paid by captains.
Group at all times under direction of Mr. Lowry, Penna. R.R.
$3.00 should cover eats and small transportation fares.
Take extra money for , cards,souviners, rides, extras.
The Banjo Band treasury pays, Hotel, RR. Fare, Boat and bus Fares.
YOU MUST OBEY Mr. LOWRY, YOUR OFFICERS AND CAPTAINS, otherwise you lose all privileges and remain in hotel room at all times.
THIS IS YOUR TRIP, YOU HELPED EARN IT, ENJOY IT TO THE GREAT-EST EXTENT, Bring your camera, Take notes, etc. HAVE THE MOST OF IT

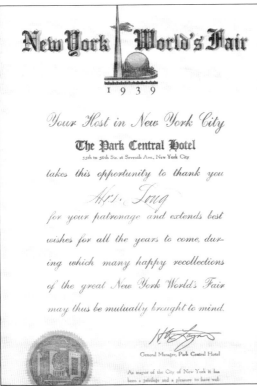

New York World's Fair

1939

Your Host in New York City

The Park Central Hotel

55th to 56th Sts. at Seventh Ave., New York City

takes this opportunity to thank you

Mrs. Long

for your patronage and extends best wishes for all the years to come, during which many happy recollections of the great New York World's Fair may thus be mutually brought to mind.

General Manager, Park Central Hotel

As mayor of the City of New York it has been a privilege and a pleasure to have wel-

During their World's Fair trip, band members stayed at the Park Central Hotel on Fifty-Fifth to Fifty-Sixth Streets. The hotel presented a parchment certificate of appreciation to each guest, including this one given to Marie Long, who accompanied the band. The certificates included the guest's name and a commemorative seal, and were signed by the general manager of the hotel and the mayor of New York.

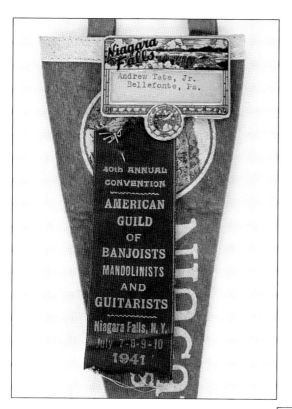

Bellefonte Banjo Band member Andrew J. Tate Jr.'s pennant and badge are pictured, along with a ribbon from the 40th annual Convention of the American Guild of Banjoists, Mandolinists, and Guitarists at Niagara Falls, New York, on July 7–10, 1941. The band took a side trip to Toronto, Ontario, while attending the convention.

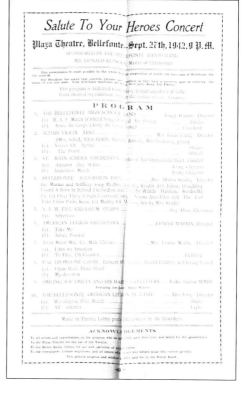

The Bellefonte High School Band, the St. John School Orchestra, the Bellefonte Accordion Band, and other performers joined with the Bellefonte Banjo Band's Salute to Your Heroes Concert on September 27, 1942, at the Plaza Theatre in Bellefonte. The concert was one of the final appearances of the band, since a growing number of male band members was going into military service.

Nine

THE GRANGE ENCAMPMENT AND FAIR

The Grange Encampment and Fair is a beloved annual event for families from throughout Centre County. Many fairgoers still spend Fair Week "tenting" in large canvas tents erected on a section of the fairgrounds, with families returning to the same tent site each year. This photograph from the early 1900s shows two men sitting on wooden rocking chairs and chatting outside of the Wesley W. Tate tent.

The Grange Fair's origins date to the years following the Civil War, when the Grange, an organization formed to advocate on behalf of farmers and rural residents, was gaining popularity across North America. In 1874, Centre Hall area resident and Grange supporter Leonard Rhone organized an annual picnic for residents to acquaint them with the Grange and to recruit new members. A few years later, some families began bringing their own tents to the picnic and opted to remain at the picnic spot overnight before returning home. This practice prompted Rhone to begin borrowing tents from the National Guard and renting them to picnic attendees. The tent pictured in these photographs was owned by W.W. Tate, and after being used as the primary tent for many years, it was repurposed as a kitchen addition set up at the rear of the primary tent.

On September 22, 1887, the *Millheim Journal* offered a description of the event: "An immense crowd of people attended the Grangers' picnic on Nittany mountain last Wednesday and Thursday. There must have been from 8,000 to 10,000 people on the ground. The Spring Mills band was among those who camped there, and they furnished the music. Over seventy tents had been struck and the exhibition of implements, furniture, organs, &c., though not very extensive, is reported to have been good. The flying horse man was there and made a little fortune, while the back drivers did a very profitable business." In early 1900s photograph at right, Teckla Tate sits on a wooden frame outside the family tent. In the photograph below from the same era, Ida Tate stands outside her tent holding flowers and a coffee pot.

Over the years, the Grange Fair has been variously known as "Grangers' Picnic," "Grange Picnic," "Grange Encampment and Fair," and informally as "The Picnic." No matter the name, children have always had a special affection for the annual event. There are always endless activities for toddlers and teenagers alike, such as livestock showing, hobby shows, enjoying the games, rides, and food on the midway, movies, dances, and much more. These two photographs show a little girl sitting on a chair at a tent and a young boy riding a pony. For older teenagers, the fair was a great place for matchmaking, with many budding romances attributed to the event.

The wooden headquarters building (now the Visitors' Information Center), adjacent to the playground at the top of the fair's main thoroughfare, has long served as the center of operations for the frenzy of fair-related activities. It serves as information center, the tent secretary's office, lost and found, a communications center, and a little bit of everything else. Prior to cell phones, fairgoers also often needed to stand in line to use the several pay phones that stood near headquarters.

The wooden Recreation Building is another of the Grange fairgrounds' traditional multipurpose buildings, featuring bare wooden floors and natural "air-conditioning" (lifting the window shutters). Generations of children and adults have passed through the "Rec" Building's doorway. Over the years, it has served as a movie theater; dance hall; meeting place for the Five Day Club (a Bible club), craft, and exercise classes; exhibit hall; and venue for magic, music, and other shows.

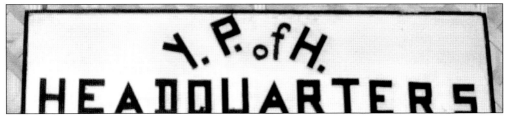

Y. P. of H.
HEADQUARTERS

This original sign hung over the Young Patrons of Husbandry headquarters on the Grange fairgrounds. The building was razed sometime after 1963. The Young Patrons of Husbandry was a Grange-affiliated group for children and young adults, with members participating in activities both at the Grange Fair and throughout the year. For example, at the June 1975 Pomona Grange meeting, it was reported that the organization had recently held a bowling party as well as a square dance at the Logan Grange Hall in Pleasant Gap.

This metal horse swing from the 1960s is one of a set of swings featuring different animals that were a fixture at the Grange Fair playground behind headquarters for years. An array of other playground equipment was also arranged throughout the area, including regular swings, seesaws, slides, a climbing frame, a merry-go-round, and sandboxes. The playground was also a popular meeting spot for teenagers.

The photograph at right, taken at the 1927 or 1928 Grange Fair, shows a young Andrew Tate Jr. standing in front of a farm machinery exhibit. Below, a daughter of Wesley W. Tate poses on top of a hay rake on the fairgrounds. Many farm machinery dealers and other related businesses would sell their implements and wares at the Grange Fair, with many farmers waiting until "fair time" to make their larger purchases since the businesses often offered Grange Fair discounts on their products and services. A section of the fairgrounds was dedicated to showing and demonstrating an assortment of farm machinery of all sizes and prices.

Families pose while visiting the fair in the 1920s. Fairgoers could drive their buggies (and later automobiles) or take the train (the railroad came through the fairgrounds) to Grange Park. The fair proved a popular destination for Centre County residents even in the horse and buggy days. For example, according to the *Millheim Journal*, the 1879 Grangers' Picnic attracted 5,000-plus attendees. The reporter noted that "the entire mountain" was seemingly "filled with people and vehicles." Since many of the attendees, including the tenters, were also farmers, someone needed to return home once or twice a day to feed the livestock and milk the cows.

The Grange Fair Premium Book is the Grange Fair bible. It contains the campground rules and regulations; lists all the departments, classes, and other information for exhibitors of livestock, produce, sewing, and other crafts and hobbies; provides detailed schedules of daily events; and more. The cover of the 94-page premium book for the 99th Grange Encampment and Fair in 1973 is shown here.

Amusement rides have been a Grange Fair midway staple since the 1910s, when the Wave, a ride owned and operated by Bellefonte resident Joseph Thal, thrilled fairgoers. From the 1930s to 1954, Reithoffer Shows provided the rides. Thereafter, Garbrick Amusements provided the rides, which included a Ferris wheel and merry-go-round purchased from Hecla Park. In this c. 1962 photograph, Barbara Roof stands in front of the swings, one of the fair's midway rides.

LEONARD RHONE
Founder of the Fair

★

A Town of Tents

Grange Fair Centennial

1874 - 1974

GEORGE McCORMICK
"Mr. Grange Fair"

FRIDAY, AUGUST 23, 1974
FAIRGROUNDS
CENTRE HALL, PA.

The Grange Fair marked its centenary in 1974 with a host of special events, including the historical pageant *A Town of Tents*, with the play's program cover shown at left. The play was written by Penn State faculty member and Livonia resident Doug Macneal, and was directed by Frank Wilson, a fellow Penn State faculty member. The cast was made up of locals. Fairgoers could purchase various mementos and souvenirs created to honor the centennial, including Styrofoam "straw" hats such as the one pictured below.

Ten

VISITING THE PAST IN PRESENT-DAY BELLEFONTE

In March 1900, plans were made for the Centre County Centennial to be held during the month of July. The following month, the Centre County Soldiers Monument and Curtin Memorial Association was organized with the goal of listing the names of all the soldiers of Centre County in every war of the nation on bronze tablets on the Diamond. A statue of Gov. Andrew Curtin was also included in the plan. The plan came to fruition, and the result is shown here.

First Presbyterian Church is on North Spring Street opposite Howard Street in downtown Bellefonte. It was organized in 1800, but the church building shown in this contemporary photograph was constructed in 1870. In 1874, the church counted 200 parishioners, with James Beaver serving as the Sunday school superintendent.

Trinity United Methodist Church on West Howard Street was built in 1876, with George W. Tate and William V. Hughes serving as contractors and designers. The church, which cost $13,500, stands on a 50-foot lot and includes two fronts on Spring and Howard Streets built of pressed brick with Reading brownstone, together with 14 stained-glass windows along both sides of the building.

St. John Catholic Church, established in 1828, stands on West Bishop Street downtown opposite the Undine Fire Company's fire hall. St. John Parochial School is housed in an adjoining building. The Servants of the Immaculate Heart of Mary served the school for 102 years before withdrawing to serve at another diocese.

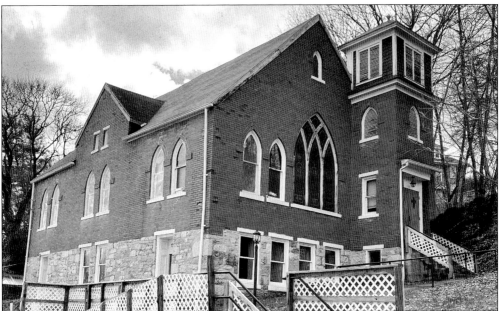

The redbrick St. Paul's African Methodist Episcopal Church, on St. Paul Street on the hillside above the Bellefonte train station, was organized in 1842. In 1874, the church reported having 36 members and 84 Sunday school scholars. The superintendent at the time was S.S. Lyon, and trustees included John Welch, M.S. Graham, J.C. Hawkins, Walter Rose (sexton), and Pastor Amos A. Williams.

John Robert Cole (1850–1916) designed the earliest buildings of the Pennsylvania Match Factory, a group of redbrick buildings west of Spring Creek adjacent to Talleyrand Park. The Pennsylvania Match Company was formed by Col. W. Fred Reynolds, J.L. Montgomery, and P.B. and F.W. Crider. The factory produced matchsticks between 1900 and 1947. It now houses the American Philatelic Society's headquarters, library, and other businesses.

The Talleyrand Park gazebo is the centerpiece of Bellefonte's 3.5-acre community park along Spring Creek. In 1974, when development of the proposed park stalled owing to financial shortfalls, the all-volunteer Talleyrand Park Committee was formed and designed the park's layout. The building of the gazebo represented a community effort, with the structure completed in time for festivities held to celebrate the nation's bicentennial in 1976.

The Plaza Theatre Building on West High Street was designed by Anna Wagner Keichline (1889–1943), a Bellefonte native and the first woman registered as an architect by the Commonwealth of Pennsylvania. The theater featured a 30-foot-by-60-foot stage, orchestra pit, and pipe organ, together with a second, smaller theater where silent movies were shown. There were 2,500 people in attendance at the theater's opening night on October 19, 1925.

The lumber firm of Millikin, Hoover & Company organized the Centre County Banking Company in 1868, with Henry Brockerhoff serving as president, John P. Harris and P. Benner Wilson and directors, and J. Dunlop Shugert as cashier. The Centre County Banking Building at 201 West High Street was designed by Bellefonte-based architect and builder George W. Tate (1822–?).

In 1889, F.W. Crider erected a new block of buildings on North Allegheny Street to replace the Humes Block. The largest business block in Centre County at that time, it was dubbed Crider Exchange. Over the years, the building has housed countless businesses and professional offices. It was also once the home of radio station WBLF, a 500-watt daytime station.

When visitors to Bellefonte step through the entrance to Plumb's Drug Store on the first level of the Crider Exchange building, they are immediately transported back in time. Some of the store's fixtures, including the illuminated Rexall Drugs sign hanging over the doorway, date to the 1950s and 1960s. An old-time soda fountain still sells sodas, malts, shakes, and other fountain favorites from the past. A luncheonette in the store's lower level closed in the mid-1960s.

The Reynolds Mansion, on Linn Street across from the former Bellefonte High School, was built in 1885 by Maj. William F. Reynolds. The home, designed by architect C.S. Wetzel, was listed in the National Register of Historic Places in 1977. The carriage house at the back of the property was built in 1893 and was once used as a chapel.

Union Cemetery on East Howard Street is the resting place of many of Bellefonte's pioneering families. With burials as early as 1808, the cemetery was chartered in 1856. Among the notable individuals in the cemetery are Evan Pugh, first president of the Pennsylvania State University; Union soldiers from Black units of the Army of the James; US senator Andrew Gregg, and Pennsylvania governors Andrew Curtin, James Beaver, and Daniel Hastings. (Earl Houser Jr.)

INDEX

BIBLIOGRAPHY

"Airmail History in Pictures, 1918–1928." about.usps.com/who-we-are/postal-history/airmail-history-in-pictures.pdf. US Postal Service, 2018.

Bellefonte: Fountain of Governors. Bellefonte Bicentenial Committee, 1976.

"Bellefonte State Fish Hatchery, Centre County." www.fishandboat.com/Fish/Stocking/StateFishHatcheries/Pages/BellefonteStateFishHatchery.aspx. Pennsylvania Fish & Boat Commission.

Bezilla, Michael. "Railroads of the Spring Creek Watershed." *The Spring Creek Watershed Atlas.* www.springcreekwatershedatlas.org/post/2020/07/25/railroads-of-the-spring-creek-watershed. Updated September 27, 2020.

Borough of Bellefonte Historic District: National Register of Historic Places Inventory—Nomination Form. Washington, DC: US National Park Service, 1977.

Butts, Charles, and Elwood S. Moore. *Geology and Mineral Resources of the Bellefonte Quadrangle, Pennsylvania.* Washington, DC: US Department of the Interior, 1936. pubs.usgs.gov/bul/0855/report.pdf.

Centre County in Pictures, 1800–1950. Bellefonte, PA: Centre County Historical Society, Centre County Sesqui-Centennial Committee, 1950.

"Correctional Facility History." centrecountypa.gov/229/History.

Dubbs, Paul M. *Where to Go and Place-Names of Centre County: A Collection of Articles from the Centre Daily Times, Compiled and Published During 1959–60.* State College, PA: Centre Daily Times, Offset Centre, and the Nittany Printing and Publishing Co., 1961.

"Freight Train Wrecks Near Bellefonte, PA." *Bristol* [TN] *Herald-Courier,* July 25, 1939, 1. newspapers.com, accessed August 8, 2021.

Linn, John Blair. *History of Centre and Clinton Counties, Pennsylvania.* Philadelphia, PA: Louis H. Everts, 1883. digital.libraries.psu.edu/digital/collection/digitalbks2/id/16140/rec/1.

Mitchell, J. Thomas. *Centre County from Its Earliest Settlement to the Year 1915.* State College, PA: Penn State University Press, 2008.

Report of the Department of Fisheries of the Commonwealth of Pennsylvania, from June 1, 1903, to November 30, 1904. Harrisburg, PA: W. Stanley Ray, State Printer of Pennsylvania, 1905.

Report of the Superintendent of Public Instruction of the Commonwealth of Pennsylvania for the year ending July 5, 1915. Harrisburg, PA: W. Stanley Ray, State Printer, 1915.

"Virtual Walking Tour of Bellefonte, Pennsylvania, A." www.bellefontearts.org/virtual_home.htm. Bellefonte Historical and Cultural Association.

DISCOVER THOUSANDS OF LOCAL HISTORY BOOKS
FEATURING MILLIONS OF VINTAGE IMAGES

Arcadia Publishing, the leading local history publisher in the United States, is committed to making history accessible and meaningful through publishing books that celebrate and preserve the heritage of America's people and places.

Find more books like this at
www.arcadiapublishing.com

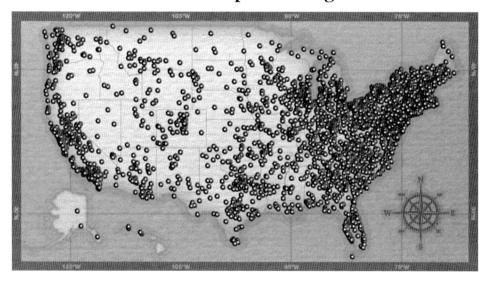

Search for your hometown history, your old stomping grounds, and even your favorite sports team.

Consistent with our mission to preserve history on a local level, this book was printed in South Carolina on American-made paper and manufactured entirely in the United States. Products carrying the accredited Forest Stewardship Council (FSC) label are printed on 100 percent FSC-certified paper.

MADE IN THE USA